From the whimsical fantasy at the beginning through Grace's heartrending true life story, *Family Secrets* is a gripping page-turner of a book. The more I read, the more I marveled at the unique way God can turn even the most horrendous tragedy into a victory. In all the years I have known Grace, I have referred to her as Amazing Grace because her life is such an example of the amazing grace of God. A must read, this book will change your life.

—Frostie Hall, author of The Dread Champions of the King adventure book series

As I began to read this book, this life story, I could not stop until I had finished every page, every story, every word. This is a gift from God that every woman should read. Your life may not even be close to Grace's, but it will open you up to yourself and what God can and will do for you. This will make you a better person by speaking to your innermost parts by revealing hidden secrets and setting you free! Praise the Lord for this open window into another's life shared with each of us. It is my honor to recommend this precious book.

—Dr. Linda L. Jones, ThD, The Praying Field Ministries

Family Secrets

Family Secrets
letters to my granddaughters

GRACE ANN NEUHARTH &
WANDA WINTERS-GUTIERREZ

Tate Publishing & *Enterprises*

Family Secrets
Copyright © 2009 by Grace Ann Neuharth & Wanda Winters-Gutierrez. All rights reserved.

This title is also available as a Tate Out Loud product. Visit www.tatepublishing.com for more information.

No part of this publication may be reproduced, stored in a retrieval system or transmitted in any way by any means, electronic, mechanical, photocopy, recording or otherwise without the prior permission of the author except as provided by USA copyright law.

The following publishers have graciously granted permission to include excerpts from their copyrighted publications.

Materials from *The Search for Peace: A Woman's Guide to Spiritual Wholeness*, by Wanda Winters-Gutierrez, copyright 2004 used by permission of Destiny Image Publishers, 167 Walnut Bottom Road, Shippensburg, PA 17257 www.destinyimage.com

Newspaper Articles from *Yankton Daily Press and Dakotan* used by permission. *Yankton Press and Dakotan*, PO Box 56, Yankton, SD 57078

Scripture quotations are taken from the *Holy Bible, King James Version*, Cambridge, 1769. Used by permission. All rights reserved.

The opinions expressed by the author are not necessarily those of Tate Publishing, LLC.

Published by Tate Publishing & Enterprises, LLC
127 E. Trade Center Terrace | Mustang, Oklahoma 73064 USA
1.888.361.9213 | www.tatepublishing.com

Tate Publishing is committed to excellence in the publishing industry. The company reflects the philosophy established by the founders, based on Psalm 68:11,
"The Lord gave the word and great was the company of those who published it."

Book design copyright © 2009 by Tate Publishing, LLC. All rights reserved.
Cover design by Amber Gulilat
Interior design by Nathan Harmony

Published in the United States of America

ISBN: 978-1-61566-133-6
1. Biography & Autobiography: Women
2. Family & Relationships: Abuse: General
09.09.14

Dedication and Thanks from Grace

I would like to dedicate this book to my Lord and Savior, who was with me every step of the way through my long journey to wholeness.

I am deeply grateful that the Lord sent along Wanda to help with this project, for she truly is a blessing to me.

I would like to thank my two daughters, who encouraged me to write the book, and my husband, who stood beside me during the process.

A special thanks to Kin and Joanna Maddox, who were first to sow financial seeds into my ministry.

With Thanks and Appreciation from Wanda

With all my heart, I want to thank God for this assignment and for entrusting me with the heart of his beautiful daughter Grace Ann Neuharth.

Grateful thanks and so much love to my children, Lisa and Nathan, Sherry and Mike, Michael and Nicole, Chris and Jeni, for always believing. You are God's greatest gift to me.

Thanks, Terry, daughter of my heart, for being who you are and doing it with such style.

To Connie, who has always been there for me.

A special gracias to Beloved... you rock my world.

We owe a great deal of gratitude to Hannah Tranberg, editor extraordinaire, cover artist Amber Gulilat and graphic designer Nathan Harmony at Tate Publishing. We so appreciate your invaluable suggestions, creative brilliance, and fine-tuning of this project.

A Word to Libby and Rylee

I began writing these letters when a friend gave me a grandmother doll holding her newborn granddaughter. The story attached to this gift related that the grandmother was a Keeper of Wisdom who by sharing her own journey helped the child become all she was meant to be. As I read it, one line struck a note in my heart.

"She saw things through Grandmother's eyes that she would not have seen unguided by a wisdom that comes only from many miles and many tears." I want to pass on to you the insights I have gained through my own many miles and many tears.

Unfortunately, my story is riddled with family secrets and is not easily told. There is no easy way to tell you about murder, suicide, abuse, depression, addictions, and slavery, but the truth is the truth, and you have a right to know. Even though there is much tragedy, my story is also rich in the ability of God to help people survive the unthinkable and more importantly move beyond survival to victory.

As I look back over my life, I am increasingly convinced that there should be no such secrets in a family. Others may not agree, but I spent too many years on the brink of a psychotic breakdown haunted by flashes of a horror movie I didn't understand. With no one to talk to I lived in an ever widening circle of lies, silence, suppression, and denial. Family secrets eventually pulled every aspect of my life into darkness.

Secrets dominated the psychological landscape of our family. Even when we were physically together, we were unable to be emotionally present for one another because everyone felt we must keep our secrets from the outside world. We lived in shame and social isolation.

Like all children who sense information is being withheld from them, I became confused and early on lost my ability to trust others. I spent the first four decades of my life wrapped in an aching misery for which I had no words. Now I have words, and I want my granddaughters to benefit from my experiences.

You have always known me as Grandma Grace who lives on a farm in Arkansas. You know I have a garden, feed the chickens, make jelly, walk in the woods, and invite people over after church to make-your-own-sundae parties. While all that may have left you with pleasant memories, it is the things you do not know about me that can change your lives.

But before we begin I want you to pretend you are still little girls and Grandma Grace is going to tell you a once upon a time story…

Before the Journey

*T*he morning dew fell gently upon the house. It was an elegant, older home with tall windows and a wide porch sweeping around the front. It appeared to be empty except for a small girl who was to be its occupant.

She had asked for a house high atop a hill, and it had been given to her by her father. She loved her house. It had many large rooms and beautiful views. Above all she loved the circular staircase. It was great fun to slide down the banister when the mood struck. The staircase was also a reminder that she would soon make a grand entrance into the world below.

One day as she wandered through her house with Father, they came to a door labeled "Necessary Room." This particular room filled her with curiosity; it was the only room whose door was closed. Hesitating, she looked at Father. He gently smiled, so she reached out and touched the knob ever so slightly. To her amazement, the door swung open.

The brightness of the room startled her. The room was filled with, what appeared to be, transparent living objects. It was if they were there, but not really. She stared in awe at their luminous beauty. She wanted to touch them to see if they were real. Each object was labeled with a small golden sign engraved in elegant script.

The first object was blue and shaped in a half round

with a point on one end. When she reached out to see how it felt, it disappeared. In confusion, she looked at Father. "It is not gone," he said. "I have deposited it deep into your heart. As long as you live, it will be there." She felt reassured and a little stronger for having reached for it. Looking down, she read the sign; it said "Survival."

The next object was a luminous yellow, like the sun. It seemed not to have a form, but its brilliance radiated so powerfully it made all the other objects in the room glow. She wondered if she dare try to hold it. Closing her eyes, she slowly reached out, and as she did, it exploded into a million tiny, iridescent rays of light. The shimmering rays went straight into her, filling every inch of her being. Reeling from the impact, she looked at the sign to see what it might have been. It simply said "The Love of God."

Amazed at all that was happening, she eagerly turned to the other items in the room. Next to the yellow object was a round pink one. Bolder now, she lay her hands on its smooth beauty, letting them rest for a moment. A feeling of warmth and serenity flowed through her from the top of her head to the soles of her feet. The pink object was "Peace."

Moving to the next table, she was surprised to see only a tiny speck. It was barely visible, but when her little finger touched its edge she felt it penetrate straight into her heart. She wondered why something so small could be so was necessary. She had to squint to read the sign; which said "Faith." She thought perhaps she would need more than a speck, but Father laughed and assured her, "Don't worry, it will grow."

There were only two objects left in the room. She

approached the crystal-clear one next; strangely it seemed to be made of many tiny pulsating slivers. In her eagerness, her hands slipped and barely glazed its surface. Having caught only a fragment, she wondered if it would be enough. The object was "Hope."

The very last one was black. Even though it was black, it had another depth of color and had the ability to change from black to an exquisite shade of red. As before, she did not read the label before reaching for the object. Eagerly grabbing it with both hands, the little girl was shocked when a burning sting shot through her heart. She had not been prepared for this, but like it or not it was now inside her. The sign read "Pain and Hurt."

Bewildered, she turned to Father and asked, "Why do I have this?" His answer was heavy with compassion. "Dear child, everyone who lives where you are going has a degree of pain and hurt; it was not my will for you to grab it with both hands, nor to experience it so early in life."

"Why did the color change from black to a pretty red?" she asked, still feeling the ache inside. "Because, my love, you have the power to change the curse into a blessing. I have given you that choice, and only you can decide if you want to change it."

"Can I change it now?" she inquired hopefully.

Father shook his head sadly. "I am sorry, little one; it cannot be changed until after the pain and hurt comes. Then you choose." She nodded her head in understanding.

Turning away from the black object, they left the room and closed the door. Walking to a window, she looked out on the valley below and studied the people. Some were happy and laughing. Some were sad. All of them were far too busy rushing here and there. She wondered why they hurried so and why they were followed by a strange darkness.

Looking farther, she saw that just above the village a translucent cloud glowed. On it was written, "I know the plans I have for you...plans to prosper you and not to harm you. Plans to give you a hope and a future" (Jeremiah 29:11).

The little girl turned to her Father. "May I see your plans for me now?"

"No, you must walk in the valley below first. As you walk through your life, I will reveal the plans."

"Now, dear child, it is time for you to go." Father spoke with love and sympathy, for he knew all too well what the valley below contained. His Son had been there for a while, and he knew about the darkness.

As the little girl and her Father walked to the staircase hand in hand, he reminded her one more time of how very much he loved her. She smiled, remembering how that love had radiated through her heart.

"Now, precious child, how do you wish to make your grand entrance into the world? You can walk down the staircase as a royal lady, or you can slide down the banister and make a big splash."

With an impish grin she answered, "Down the banister, if you please!"

And Father gave her a gentle push.

There are years that ask questions and years that answer.
   —*Zora Neale Hurston*

*D*ear *G*randdaughters,

*I*magine you were four years old and life as you knew it suddenly evaporated. My story begins there. I was riding in a car and as we pulled into the driveway a blinding ray of sunlight shot through the window making me squint. When I turned my head away from its brightness I realized I had no idea where I was or how I got there. I did not recognize the boy sitting beside me, nor did I know the people in the front seat of the car. I didn't even know my own name. Nothing. My memory bank was completely wiped out.

The car stopped and I could tell I was expected to get out, but was too scared to move. The boy in the backseat appeared to be about my age or maybe a little older. He smiled and nudged me to get out of the car. I stared at him numb with fear. I had not noticed the man get out of the front seat and was startled when the door on my side of the car suddenly sprang open. The man reached for my arm, and as he did his jacket opened just enough for me to catch sight of a gun. I tried to scream, *Who are you people? What is this place? How did I get here?* but no words came. The man with the gun pulled me out and led me into the house. My mind spun trying to figure it all out. The only thought that came to me was that I had been kidnapped.

Once inside, the couple disappeared into another room. I turned and headed for the door, but the boy blocked my path, staring at me without saying a word. Like a trapped animal, I glared at him briefly to see if he would move out of my way. When he didn't, I quickly scanned the strange room for another way out. There was none.

I'm not sure where I learned to pray, but standing there, my stomach a burning knot of fear, I sent up a desperate plea. "God, please help me. Help me and help Mommy and Daddy find me so I can go home."

My memory did not begin to return for nearly thirty years.

---

*D*ear *L*ibby and *R*ylee,

A simple definition of stress is when life comes at you faster than you can cope. I had hit my limit. It would be a long time before the mental health field came up with a name for what happened that day. The experts now say post traumatic stress disorder (PTSD) is a serious condition that can manifest after a person has experienced or witnessed a traumatic or terrifying event in which serious physical harm occurred or was threatened.

Over the years, I have experienced many PTSD-type symptoms other than loss of memory, including guilt of something unknown, emotional numbness, relationship issues, depression, disassociation, hopelessness, suicidal tendencies, serious illnesses, and terrifying flashbacks.

There is a test they use to measure the degrees of stress people go through before they are in danger of running into serious problems physically or mentally. A score of 250 within a year is considered high. Different life situations contribute to the bottom line. For instance, the death of a parent is 101, change in living conditions is 42, and change of residence is 40. By the time my memory crashed my total life change score had climbed to well over a 1000, all within a six month period.

I was four years old when every vestige of my life was stripped away. It was as if someone had closed off the portion of my mind that stored all the information about my identity, and everything else that had happened to me up until this point. I had no name, no past, no one, and nothing to cling to. My world was suddenly filled with strangers and secrets.

The Bible says, "Whatsoever a man thinks in his heart so is he." That is exactly how it was for me. For the next twelve years, I settled into life with the strangers I believed were kidnappers. For many of those years, I never gave up praying my real mom and dad would come to get me. In the meantime, I emotionally detached from the people in the house. I was unsure of the adults' identities. I thought the boy, they called David, was their birth son. They called me Marilyn Sue, and I hated it. I knew only two things: my name was not Marilyn Sue, and I did not belong with these people.

I melted into this situation the best I could, but I always felt as if I were trying to remember something just on the tip of my tongue. I tried so very hard to reconcile what my subconscious mind knew with what my conscious mind either could not remember or would not accept. I spent long, frustrating hours staring off into space trying to access it, whatever 'it' was, but I could not.

There was a strange paradox at work in my mind. On one hand I wanted to know about my life before, but when certain memories threatened to surface, I protected myself from the pain of remembering in many ways. One escapism was humming, especially during mealtimes.

This inner back-and-forth dance of trying to remember and at the same time protecting myself from those very memories took so much out of me I had little emotional energy left to pay attention to what was happening in the house. Therefore much of everyday life never made it into my conscious memory bank.

Over the years a few recollections of living with my kidnappers did slip past my disassociation. Many of them were simple everyday details of family life, innocent and sometimes humorous, still other things left me terrorized, guilt ridden, and helpless.

I see these incidents in fragments, so that is how I will relate them to you. The first house I was taken to was a one-story with three bedrooms and one bath. It sat on a tree-lined street and had a huge bay window in the kitchen just above the kitchen sink. In the back corner of the kitchen was a booth similar to that of a restaurant. I cannot describe the rest of the house or for that matter what my room looked like.

The first year I do not recall seeing much of my captors. This was probably because James had been called up to active duty in the army due to the Korean War. He was, however, stationed stateside and lived at home. Marilyn worked the graveyard shift.

Our daily care was given over to an older lady. She had a sweet, soft face surrounded by a halo of gray hair. I felt safe with her. She prepared all of our meals, including supper, before going to her own home at night. She was the first grandmother figure I remember. Her hugs and kindness made my confused loneliness bearable.

Tuesdays with Grandmother were special. Shortly after breakfast, she would pack sack lunches for herself, David, and me then we'd walk to the corner and catch a bus to her church. While she worked on things to send to missionaries, we played with other children. At noon the group broke for lunch, and everyone ate together.

I remember when the boy broke his collarbone. We were playing tag, and he ran hard into the corner of the house. Our caretaker got him to the doctor, and during the examination they discovered he was legally blind in one eye. He hadn't even seen the house.

In September, both of us started school. I was in kindergarten and David in first grade. One of the few times I remember Marilyn was in connection with the scene she made because they had not given me the teacher she wanted me to have. When she got through with the principal, I was moved to a different class. I learned that day that she had a way of getting what she wanted.

We took public transportation to and from school, so each morning we were given two nickels each. The boy received orders to come by my classroom after school and help me get on the correct bus. On the first day, he stopped by my room and announced that for some reason we had to walk home from school; furthermore, I was to turn my nickel over to him. This same scenario took place three days in a row until I caught on that he just wanted my money. So on the fourth day when he showed up and made his usual speech asking for my nickel. I said, "Since I have to walk home anyway, I spent my nickel at lunch for an ice cream bar." I may have had some problems, but being dumb was not one of them.

The boy was furious that I dared to do such a thing when I should have saved that money for him. We were still arguing when my captors came home. They had no patience for children bickering, so from that day on there were no more nickels for the bus. We had to walk both to and from school.

Other memories are not so benign. One day while I was on the playground at school, a little girl showed me a wind-up duck that belonged to her handicapped brother. She wound up the toy and placed it on the ground. I stooped down and picked it up to get a closer look, but when it started vibrating in my hand I dropped it on the asphalt and it broke. The girl started screaming at me, "That belongs to my sick brother! This is going to just kill him that you broke it! He is just going to die, and it's your fault!"

The phrase "this is going to kill" struck a nerve in my subconscious. As I backed away in confusion, a tape played through my head: "dead…it's your fault…it's your fault…it's your fault…you killed…dead!"

My heart pounded in my chest as my mind raced quickly going into overdrive trying to access information. "Dead…kill." Where had I had heard that before? She was still screaming at me as I ran toward the swing sets grabbing the first one available. The hypnotic back-and-forth movement soothed the overpowering feelings I didn't understand. I knew something that I really didn't know, but what? *What?* I lost track of time trying to figure it out, and when I looked up, no one else was on the playground. All the other kids had heard the recess whistle blow and gone back to class. I was all alone.

There was something else that happened about this time in 1951 or '52. The radio was playing a song called the "Tennessee Waltz," and I was dancing around in my own make-believe world when all of a sudden the music stopped and a voice made an announcement that someone had died. I stopped twirling and stood still; someone died. It seemed like an announcement I had heard before. My dance had been interrupted by death.

    People getting killed and dying haunted me. Strange, shadowy ghosts without form moved through my daydreams and stole into my sleep. Danger seemed to always be near. Little did I know that the threat of my own murder was a coming reality.

---

*D*ear *G*irls,

*M*y captors were not all they appeared to be. Like many people they had a public side and a private side. All of us generally put our best foot forward to the outside world, but in this case the hidden side of their lives was far darker than anyone could imagine.

Marilyn was a religious person who had been a part of different ministries when she was younger. She had many friends who thought the world of her. Besides being a chauffeur for a famous woman evangelist, she was also gifted in music and could play any instrument by ear.

While other people could see her gifts and potential, I was left to deal with the reality of what she became. By the time she and James got me, all music had left her life and she was a woman full of unresolved issues on the brink of self-destruction. This was not visible to the vast majority of their friends and family because she worked very hard to make everything picture perfect.

Soon after I arrived, she insisted that the boy and I be, as she called it, "dedicated to the Lord." In the photograph I have commemorating this special event we looked like two life-size dolls. My blond curls are in place, I am dressed in a red and white striped blouse, and my red jumper had trim to match the blouse. My socks are red with white trim, and I am wearing new white shoes. In one hand I hold a red purse and a white sweater. David looks polished and grownup in his gray suit, white shirt, and red tie. He has a little white handkerchief tucked into his breast pocket. His shoes are white with brown tips.

After doing her motherly duty and dressing us up in the latest fifties style, she took us to one of her friend's home. Parking us on the couch with the warning to not get messed up, she turned to her friend and said, "Ask the pastor to dedicate them to the Lord at the end of service, and in case I don't make it back, just go ahead and have them dedicated anyway. You can stand in for me," and out the door she went.

I don't remember ever being at this church before, but there we were watching all these babies getting dedicated. When the pastor called us forward, I felt embarrassed that we were so much older. The lady started leading us up the aisle when suddenly Marilyn slipped in the back door and followed us to the platform. I was not too happy about having a bunch of people staring at me, but it lasted all of five minutes, and when it was over she slipped back down the aisle and left the building. We went home with the lady and were picked up later in the day. In her religious zeal, she missed the point of dedicating children to the Lord, especially the part about loving them, protecting them, and vowing to raise them in a godly home.

On the surface, James had a gentle way that drew people to him. His many friends, as well as the men he worked with on the police force, would have sworn that he was above reproach. All the good-old-boy clichés fit him to a tee. He was considered "the salt of the earth," a "fine family man" devoted to his wife and children. Not only that, he was the best possible neighbor.

One of the families who lived near us had a cabin in the mountains at Arrowhead. James would take the boy and me, as well as the neighbors' kids, up there by himself to spend a week at a time. The parents were mightily impressed, and the kids told them they had a fine time. He regaled us with stories about being in the navy during World War II. Although his ship was out on maneuvers at the time, he was stationed in Hawaii when the Japanese bombed Pearl Harbor.

In the evening he'd have everyone write stories, or he would start a story, and everyone added a line until we ended up with a hilarious tale. Yes, indeed, James Hoskins was a fine man, but behind the walls of our house it was a different story.

The sexual abuse started when I was very young, too young to know what it was and too terrified to tell. One day when everyone else was out of the house, he told me to come into his room and lay on his bed with him. When I hesitated, he said, "I am your daddy now, and if you don't want to end up like your mother, you better just do what I tell you to do."

His words frightened me, and I started to pull away. That's when I saw the knife lying on the nightstand. Something about its long, shiny blade tore at my insides, making me sick to my stomach. As he pulled me into the bed, I begged, "No! Please, I want to go back to my room. I'm getting sick." I hear myself repeating, "No...I'm sick...please, no," but he wouldn't listen. As he continued, all I could think was, *Knife...like your mother...don't tell...knife...end up like your mother.*

Again, I had no idea why the sight of that knife and those words had such a terrifying effect on me. But James knew.

He had found a sure-fire way to keep me quiet and render me emotionally helpless while he satisfied his demons.

Another time, Marilyn was out cold in their bedroom, having taken her usual sleeping pills after coming home from work. David had gone to visit a friend. It was our caretaker's day off. James had worked in the den all morning while I entertained myself. Early in the afternoon, he called me into the room and motioned for me to come over to him where he lay on the couch. With dread, I made my way across the room knowing what was coming. He pulled me down beside him and slipped his hand inside my panties. When he said, "You know, I should just get a knife and cut this off; you don't need it anyway," my mind shut down.

Over the years, the threat of that knife was always present. Until I left that house at seventeen, I lived with the surety that if I didn't keep his secret I would be mutilated or murdered.

---

*D*ear *G*irls,

About three years after I came to live with the Hoskins, they moved into another house. I lost my sweet grandmother-type caregiver. Marilyn's cousin and her husband came to live with us. The cousin did all the housework and cooking. James and Marilyn continued doing whatever. The boy and I were left to our own devices.

Of all the places we lived, this house was my favorite. I was especially fond of the curving staircase and old-fashioned windows. There was a pond out back where two ducks lived and raised a family. Although the house was large, the boy and I shared a room. In one of our walls was a curious recess about two feet off the floor. It was in the shape of a little house approximately three feet wide, four deep, and with a pitched ceiling about three feet high at its highest point. I quickly claimed this nook as my sanctuary and spent many hours curled up in my house, coloring and working jigsaw puzzles.

Early on, I had become fascinated with puzzles. Perhaps I was trying to make the pieces of my life fit together into a pretty picture. Undisturbed in this special place, I finished a lot of puzzles. However, the pieces of my life took years and years to fit into place and years and years more before they made a pretty picture.

With no memory and little normal interaction from adults, I had to learn many things the hard way. For instance, no one told me that the heat vents in the floors of our house got very hot. I got that message one night after I got out of the tub and stepped on the floor register to get warm. I quickly stepped off but not before the grate had burned a waffle pattern on the soles of my feet.

Another painful experience was learning to ride a bike. Libby, I can't help but contrast my experience to what your mother wrote to me when you learned to ride. She said you were about four years old when they bought you your first bicycle. It was purple and pink with purple and white streamers coming out of the handlebars. Your daddy taught you to ride by first taking you to a grassy spot and having you practice getting on by yourself. Since your bicycle did not have training wheels, he then took you out on the street and held onto the back of the bike for a while as you pedaled madly. Once in a while he let go, always running closely behind; if you tipped, he caught you. He did this a couple of times up and down the road until you were able to go all by yourself with no one holding on. When you really got the hang of it, your mom, dad, and the other kids clapped and cheered your triumph. It only took you one day.

In our new neighborhood, all the kids ran around on bikes, and we felt left out of all the fun. David begged for months for a bike, but James and Marilyn rarely paid attention to us, so after a while, he gave up. I'm not sure what finally got through to them, perhaps the pressure that a good old boy's kids needed a bike like the rest of the children, but at any rate, one day, two brand-new bikes were presented to us.

I was speechless. There in the glow of the afternoon sun was the prettiest red bike I had ever seen. It was full size, not small like the other kids rode. Awed, I reached out and touched the shiny chrome of the handlebars. I never dreamed I would have a bike, much less one this beautiful. Finally finding my voice, I asked, "How do you ride it?"

The answer came as James disappeared into the house. "Just hop on and start pedaling as fast as you can," he said as the screen door slammed. He had done his duty as a good family man and bought bikes for his kids. The rest was up to us.

The boy caught on quickly, but my bike was far too big for me, and it did not have training wheels. But hopping on and pedaling fast sounded doable, so without hesitation, I hopped on and promptly fell over. Realizing this might not be as easy as it sounded, my stubborn streak kicked in, and I decided I would learn to ride this bike with or without help.

I had never even ridden a tricycle and had no idea what I was doing, but with sheer determination, I stayed with it hours on end, day after day, sweat pouring down my face. After three days, I could still only pedal one-half a rotation before the bike tilted. My frustration level rose by the moment, but finally after two solid weeks, the concept of balancing hit me. Another week and I had it! I could ride a bike!

When a bunch of kids came riding up the road, I jumped on my bike without hesitation and joined them. I felt proud of my accomplishment and for a few minutes sailed along in glorious victory. Then we hit a steep hill, and I was in trouble. Keeping up with them took everything I had and more. Gasping for air, I pedaled with all my might, telling myself over and over, "I can make it... I can make it."

At the top of the hill, I lost all control on the speed and

realized too late I didn't know how to slow down. No one had told me about brakes. My heart pounded harder and harder as the bike raced erratically down the hill, gaining speed with each passing second. Soon the once smooth road became rough and littered with rocks. Suddenly, I flew over the handlebars and landed hard in a pile of broken glass. My knees and hands were lacerated, full of slivered glass, gravel, asphalt, and dirt.

Dragging my bike and myself to the side of the road, I sat there bawling while I picked debris out of my knees. The other kids were long gone, and no one else was around, so I limped home pushing the bike. At the house, I cleaned my wounds and removed the rest of the glass piece by piece. After applying a bandage, I sat alone in my little house, wounded hands and knees aching. There was no one to tell, no one to comfort me.

This next incident is classic of how adrift I was. The year I was in sixth grade, notices were sent home with the girls that they were going to have a talk on Friday night about something called periods. In order to attend, you had to have an adult present with you. I took the note home, but Marilyn could not go, so that was that.

About a year later, I began my period and was completely clueless as to what was happening. I just knew that I was bleeding. I was too much of a loner to ask the other girls what was happening, so I reasoned that since I was in no pain maybe this was a normal part of life. I went to the bathroom and waded up toilet paper and stuck it in my underwear so as not to get blood on my clothes. This continued for six months until one day Marilyn was putting something in the dirty clothes hamper and noticed some stains on my panties. When she asked if I had started my period, I replied, "I don't know. At certain times of the month I bleed."

She told me to come into the den where she picked up the phone and dialed a number. After speaking to someone, she handed me the receiver and said, "This is a female evangelist, and she will tell you about your period." She then walked out of the room. After a bit, she returned with the supplies I needed, set them on the desk, and we never discussed the matter again.

Besides the lack of mothering and the sexual abuse, the utter loneliness of my entire existence added to my ongoing torment. Unfortunately, it got worse.

*D*ear *G*irls,

*M*edical science has determined that traumatic, stressful events may trigger a biological process that can contribute to the onset of disease. There is also a well-documented study stating that keeping secrets will affect your immune system and leave you susceptible to illnesses. All the traumas in my past that I didn't remember, as well as the things that were happening with James that I remembered all too well and kept secret finally took its toll. I was eight years old when my body gave out on me.

The school I attended was a block and a half from the house. It was usually an easy walk for me, but for the past two weeks I had not been well. Marilyn's cousin took me to see the doctor, but he found nothing wrong, so I had to keep going to school. On this particular morning, I felt like I was moving through a thick fog.

Told to stop dawdling, I picked up my sack lunch in one hand, my books in the other, and headed out the door. I got just past our next-door neighbors' house when my knees gave way. My lunch and books scattered in all directions. I tried to pull myself up but was unable to stand. It took an hour for me to crawl inch by inch the thirty feet back to the house. I had to stop every few minutes to rest. Finally, I dragged myself up the three steps, opened the door, and collapsed unconscious on the living room floor.

I woke up on an examination table in the doctors' office. As I was coming to, I heard the doctor say, "There is no need for any blood work to be done. I can tell just by looking at her what is wrong; she has jaundice." Someone nearby insisted on the blood work anyway.

The doctor left the room and sent in a lab technician to draw some blood. My arms were very small, and the tech poked and poked looking for a vein. It took five tries before he found one; by then I was crying in fear and pain. The needle hurt, but the sight of blood being drained from my body was dreadful in a way I couldn't explain. Still crying, I watched transfixed as the technician put a small dab of blood on litmus paper. Then he did something unthinkable; he poured my blood down the drain. As I watched the red stream flow from his fingers I began to cry louder, this time in anger. *How dare he pour out blood! How dare he pour out my blood!* Of course, my emotional reaction was all out of proportion to the incident.

When the doctor came back, he reported that it was just as he had suspected. "She has a type of yellow jaundice called infectious hepatitis." He prescribed medication and sent me home for complete bed rest. Because it was contagious, the rest of the inhabitants of the house would have to get gamma globulin shots.

My bed was moved downstairs to the dining room for the duration of my illness. I had only enough energy to feed myself one meal a day; the rest of the time I was spoon fed. Eventually the school district supplied a teacher who came to the house one day a week for several hours. She taught me the bare necessities of what I needed to know in order to pass the third grade.

My recovery dragged on and on. I had gotten sick close to Thanksgiving and remained bedfast past Christmas,

New Year's, and beyond. By bailing out on me, my body was actually protecting itself from the abuse. During my illness the incidents with James were suspended because there were too many people around.

By spring I began to feel better, and on Easter morning I was allowed out of bed for a while. I even ventured in the backyard for the first fresh air I had breathed in months. It felt so clean and fresh, just like the air after a rain. I was still not well enough to play, but with each new day my strength returned.

About that time, some friends of Marilyn's stopped by for a visit on their way to start a church in Florida. My strongest memory of that day was of the lady and the beautiful gold skirt she was wearing. I was mesmerized with how it swished and swirled, caught the light, and glowed as she moved gracefully around the room. At that age I thought I was ugly, and I just knew if I had a skirt like that I would be beautiful like the lady. At that moment, I wanted a gold skirt more than anything in the world.

This vision of loveliness took a particular interest in both David and me. She talked to us at length about the plans she and her husband had of starting a church in a seaside resort. Then she turned to James and Marilyn and said, "Say, why don't you let us take the children for a while? It will be a vacation for them!" Before they could answer, she turned backed to us and asked if we would like to go.

David said, "Sure!" and I asked, "Can I have a skirt like yours?" She was quick to reply that I could have all the gold skirts I wanted if both of us came along with them on their adventure. Marilyn and James declared me not fully recovered enough to be going anywhere. Then the beautiful lady said they would be glad to take the boy by himself. Again, the answer was no; they would not allow us to be separated for any length of time.

Unable to talk James and Marilyn into changing their minds, the couple left, and I never saw them again. A year or so later, their picture appeared in the papers. They had indeed gone to Florida and started a church. But my beautiful lady in the gold skirt began to tell people that she was Mary and would be giving birth to the Messiah. Many people gave them money for the sole purpose of having the Messiah, and his mother, bless them. When the promised Messiah did not materialize, their church members got disenchanted and turned them into the authorities. They were convicted of fraud.

Overhearing Marilyn and James talking about them, I found out that the lady could not have children and perhaps the reason for wanting us to go along with them was so that the boy could pose as the Messiah everyone was expecting. So David missed his opportunity to be a deity, and I never did get a beautiful gold skirt.

*D*ear *G*irls,

I went out to the garden today and pulled up all the garlic. The bulbs are out on the screened porch drying. Also picked green beans and brought in three heads of cabbage for the freezer. Rylee, do you remember how you used to help me snap green beans after I took off both ends?

All these domestic chores got me to thinking about the person who first taught me about keeping house and cooking. From time to time in the early years, we were allowed to stay with Marilyn's mother and father for the weekend. They became true grandparents to us. Grandma always seemed older than her years because in her thirties her hair had turned prematurely white. She was tall and carried her weight in all the right places, but the beautiful part of her was the always present, warm smile.

Grandpa was quite a contrast to Grandma. He was on the short side and somewhat round. One of the first things I noticed about Grandpa was his teeth. He had none. He always claimed he had a set in his drawer but they were too uncomfortable to wear. Nevertheless he could still eat steak with the best of them.

When you stepped into their apartment, you couldn't help but notice the beautiful coffee table, end tables, and telephone bench that Grandpa had made. He had also built a little chair that sat in the corner holding Grandma's one-hundred-year-old porcelain doll. She wore a long lace dress and had a delicate painted face. If I was really careful, I could hold her for short periods of time.

I slept on the sofa in the living room. It had crocheted doilies on the arms and back held firmly in place with straight pins. In the middle of the coffee table sat the family Bible. This big black book was a statement to Grandma's strong faith. She was very particular that nothing was ever placed on top of the Word of God, for it was holy and must not be defiled.

Curled up on the couch in this cozy setting, I watched hours and hours of Westerns on television. There was Roy Rogers and Dale Evans, Hopalong Cassidy and the Cisco Kid, but my favorite was the Lone Ranger. His mask intrigued me, but I loved the fact that he rescued people from the bad guys.

Having survived the Great Depression, Grandma became very conservative. She was the personification of the Depression-era jingle "Use it up, wear it out, make it do, or do without." She was into recycling and the green movement long before it was cool. In the interest of conservation, I could have only have two inches of water in the tub for my bath when I visited. "That is sufficient to clean anybody" was her no-nonsense declaration.

I loved to watch Grandma do her housework. She moved with an easy elegance that made housekeeping look simple. Her day began by folding the bedcovers back until all the sheets were exposed. Then she opened the bedroom windows, letting them air out until precisely ten o'clock, when she would come back into the room and make up the beds. Although I appreciated Grandma's artistic grace in housekeeping, it never rubbed off on me. I just clean house because somebody has to do it.

She was also a wonderful cook. Grandpa's rotund belly

was proof that everything she made was delicious. One of my favorite dishes was her chicken and noodles. She made them for me every time I visited. And her fresh green beans were memorable! Early in the morning she would take the ends off, snap them in half then throw them into a pot, along with onions and bacon strips. They would then be allowed to simmer on the back of the stove for most of the day. When the scent permeated the house, you knew you were in for a treat.

Saturday mornings we took the trolley to town. While there she went to her weekly beauty shop appointment and then made the rounds to pay her bills. She thought that a person should pay their bills in person rather than mailing them. Perhaps the high price of postage had something to do with it. Stamps were three cents each in 1952, and of course Grandma pinched a penny until Mr. Lincoln felt it.

On Sunday, we dressed up in our nicest clothes for church. Grandma always wore face powder and sometimes fluffed some on my upturned face. Before we left the apartment, she'd slip a red foil package of Sen-Sen into her purse. This was an old-time breath mint from the fifties, which consisted of tiny pieces of licorice with a very strong flavor. Grandma used them so often that the scent of Sen-Sen is always mingled with memories of her. Although he didn't stay, Grandpa took us to church and picked us up afterwards. He preferred spending Sunday mornings in his workshop.

The physical structure of Grandma's church was unusual. It was built on top of a hill. The concrete steps that led up to the entrance were so wide that three handrails were installed to accommodate everyone walking up the steps. Every time I attended that church, I counted the steps. There were exactly twenty-two steps to the front door.

Once inside, we separated to attend our individual classes. There is one Sunday-school lesson that I remember to this day. The lesson was about the city of refuge. Both Moses and Joshua had established places of refuge for those people who accidentally caused the death of another person. As I remember it, the roads that led to these cities had to be kept in good repair and remain open at all times. The cities of refuge were never more than thirty miles apart. Anyone could easily make it there in a day's time.

These cities were provided to protect a person from revenge seekers until the case could be judged. If the person was found innocent and remained under the protection of the city, he would be safe. If, however, he chose to wander around outside the area of protection, then he was fair game for anyone who wished to kill him.

As the teacher taught this lesson, I sat on the edge of my seat, listening intently to every word she spoke. I felt for some reason I must hang on to this story because I was going to need it. At the same time I wondered, *Why would I need a city of refuge? Whose death could I be responsible for? Was that why James threatened to kill me with the knife? Was I already guilty?* There were too many unanswered questions for one little girl. All I knew was I would need a city of refuge. The next few years proved that insight to be all too true.

*D*ear *G*irls,

*T*he last place I lived in with my captors was a three-bedroom tract house located in a newly developed subdivision where every fourth home was identical. These days we call them cookie-cutter houses. In these picture-perfect little places families lived the American Dream and *Leave It to Beaver* lives. Mothers wore ruffled aprons and stayed home, and daddies went to work. On weekends, daddies cooked out on the grill and played catch with their sons while mommies taught daughters to make potato salad and bake brownies.

Of course, that does not describe us. Whatever the opposite of normal was, we were it. By this time, nothing in our lives was typical. No mommy in the kitchen. No daddy who wanted to play normal games. No vacations. No trips to the park. No going to the beach, although it was only twenty miles away. No milk and cookies after school. No help with homework.

For the first time we did not have outside help. Marilyn's cousin and her husband had moved into their own place, and it was decided that at eleven and ten years old, the boy and I no longer needed a babysitter. Within a few days of moving into the American Dream, it was apparent that something was seriously missing. Meals were not prepared. Clothes were not washed. The house was not cleaned. This all became intolerable to Marilyn. However, it was not intolerable enough to persuade her to put on a ruffled apron and do the work. I received that assignment.

My "chores," as they liked to call them, included

everything pertaining to the running of the house. I was expected to wash the clothes, hang them on the line, and, because this was years before permanent press, iron them after they dried.

I did the household shopping and prepared all the meals. The housework included dusting, vacuuming, scrubbing toilets, and general picking up of any mess being left behind by others. Once a week, I washed windows. Thanks to Grandma, I knew a little something about cooking and cleaning.

It was at this time that I began to see how fragile Marilyn was emotionally. I also discovered that she was an addict. While cleaning the house, I found an enormous amount of drugs in her nightstand. She took sleeping pills when she came home from work and gulped down something called yellow jackets when she got up. There were other bottles with no labels. She kept a hypodermic needle in her jewelry box.

Since we had moved at the end of the school year, I spent all summer doing nothing but chores. I really tried to do everything Marilyn expected, but I lacked the maturity and the temperament. There was never any praise and no slack cut for my young age. There was no pleasing her. Her typical response was one of criticism that seemed to flow from a deep well of seething anger. Her corrections were always delivered inches from my face, her eyes narrowed as she screamed, "Marilyn Sue, you forgot to vacuum under the couch again! I purposely left a dated piece of paper under there two days ago and it's still there!"

While she ranted, I stood silent, eyes averted, as she

wrapped up her tirade with the litany I was to hear over and over for the next six years.

"My nerves are shot! One of these days I am going to kill myself, and it will be your fault! Do you get that? Your fault!"

Telling any ten-year-old that she holds someone else's life in her hands is an unfair responsibility. Delivering that kind of edict into the fragile psyche of a child who had gone through what I had was devastating. She said it so often and so forcefully I came to the place where I believed with all my heart that if I didn't do everything perfectly it would kill her. It scared me. I thought I had been afraid before, but this was different. This dread rose out of an unknown place and lodged in my throat like a lump of ice that wouldn't melt.

I became paranoid where Marilyn was concerned. When she was around, my eyes darted constantly from her face to the rooms around us, searching, always searching to see if there was anything I had left undone that might upset her. Her every movement became a gauge that declared me guilty or innocent.

Torn between anger at being a slave and the fear of what would happen if I stopped caused me to constantly weigh every decision I made. Deciding to sweep something under a rug or not dust that day became life-and-death decisions. I had to choose between my life and the way I wanted it to be and weigh that against Marilyn's death. Ultimately, in resignation, I retreated into myself and did whatever it took to save Marilyn's life.

Along the way, I took on the misconception that everyone was like Marilyn. I walked on eggshells so I wouldn't upset people. This included clerks in stores, teachers, delivery men, kids at school. This mind-set was so embedded in me that on the rare occasions we went out to eat at a restaurant and the waitress asked me what I wanted, I'd drop my head and say, "Anything...it don't matter." I was afraid that I might order something wrong and if they didn't have it on the menu or were out of it, the waitress might kill herself. I couldn't take the chance. I learned to not have an opinion on anything. I now know how ridiculous that sounds. Back then it wasn't funny.

For years and years, even after growing up, I felt solely responsible for making sure everyone around me had some degree of happiness in their lives. Not a good way to live. In fact it was no life at all, laying the life God gave me, my free will, who I really was, on the sacrificial altar of someone else's life. I discovered there are many ways to die; sometimes you are still walking around.

In addition to performing the household duties, there was always that other "duty." James began again to come into my room late at night. During the day I would catch a certain look in his eyes and know what he had in mind. I lived in dread. There was no way I could tell Marilyn. I figured that if she threatened to kill herself over a streak I left in the sliding glass door she really would do herself in right then and there if she knew what James was doing.

In the fall, I entered fifth grade, and in addition to my usual chores, I had to go to school, do my homework, and get reasonably good marks. Marilyn continued to work, come home, take sleeping pills, go to bed, get up, pop more pills, do house inspections, and scream that "her nerves were shot and I would be the death of her." James continued doing what he did every chance he got. The boy was allowed to have freedom to play and have friends.

I lived in two worlds—the outward world of an abused child keeping secrets out of fear and the inner world of a kidnap victim praying for my mommy and daddy to come get me. I longed to be safe with my mother, for I knew that she loved me dearly. My dream mother was like other mothers who cooked and cleaned and talked to me and let me play with other kids, and she would never allow anything bad to happen to me. It was only a dream, but it was all I had.

*D*ear *L*ibby and *R*ylee,

*A*s the year progressed, I became a virtual prisoner to James and Marilyn's mental and physical control. Except for school and going to the grocery store, I almost never ventured out of the house and never alone. When I timidly asked permission to go somewhere I was told, "No, you haven't finished your chores." The weekend visits to Grandma and Grandpa's ended when we moved. I had no friends. Visitors to our house were few and far between. We rarely went to see other people. So it was a total surprise when a new family came into our lives.

They were a family of six. The mother had flaming red hair like Marilyn's, but there the resemblance ended. This lady was a loving and caring mother with a marvelous sense of humor. Her sparkling eyes and laughter saturated a room with happiness. David and I were introduced as her niece and nephew. Marilyn called the newcomer Sis, although I had never heard Grandma mention another daughter. It was not in me to ask questions and not in Marilyn to volunteer an answer, so I let it lie.

Several times we traveled the seventy miles to visit Aunt Martha and her family. It was a real treat to have a reprieve from my chores and James's visits. But even as I played with the other kids I knew I was being watched. More than once I looked up to see James standing at the door staring at me. He need not have worried. I was too scared to tell his secrets. His threats and the hunting knife were never far from my mind.

On one visit we were playing outside when Martha's

daughter took me aside and said, "You do know that my mom is not your real aunt, don't you?" When I shook my head no, she continued, "My mother and you are really cousins. We just have to pretend that she is your aunt for them." I did not have time to ask for details, because the adults had made their way into the backyard.

I had no idea what she was talking about, but true to form, I asked no questions. After a while it didn't matter; whoever she was, I loved her. My lonely, motherless heart was drawn to Martha like a magnet. During our visits I silently watched her with shy, adoring eyes. Just being near her I could feel her love.

One day I got up the nerve to say, "Aunt Martha, its wonderful how you cook meals while the children play." When she looked perplexed, I stammered, "I wish we could come for Thanksgiving dinner." Martha gave me a sweet smile and said she would ask. It was hard not to cry when they said no, but I had learned that tears, or any show of emotion was, not tolerated. It was many years before I unlearned that lesson.

Our so-called family had little in common with the rest of the world. In my captors' house most holidays and all birthdays were skipped. Every year the kids at school got really excited about Thanksgiving. Once in art class we made turkey pictures by tracing our open hand, coloring the fingers like feathers, and drawing a beak on the thumb. Our teacher said we could decorate our Thanksgiving table with our project. I knew better.

After Martha's invitation was turned down, I resigned myself to making one of my standard dishes for dinner, hot dogs with macaroni and cheese. It would be just another day. But early Thanksgiving morning I answered a knock at the door, and, to my speechless delight, Aunt Martha stood there with a huge uncooked turkey in her arms. The children filed in laughing and giggling carrying sacks of groceries. After plopping the turkey on the countertop, she shooed us all out of the kitchen and set to work.

I was so happy that day. Wonderful aromas floated through the house while I played games with the other kids. I was living my dream. For a few short hours, all the ugly words and the pain went away. For a few short hours I was a normal little girl, and in the kitchen a mommy was cooking for her family.

When Martha called us to eat, the sight of the table took my breath away. She had prepared a feast beyond my wildest imagination. There, spread out in all its spectacular glory, was a Thanksgiving to beat all Thanksgivings. It had it all: a golden brown turkey and savory stuffing, creamy mashed potatoes with giblet gravy, ruby red cranberry sauce and piles of fluffy, homemade yeast rolls. She had even cooked the green beans with bacon and onions like Grandma. On the countertop sat three perfectly baked pumpkin pies and a bowl of real whipped cream.

It was the kind of lovely memory that burned clearly and sharply into my soul to be savored again and again. I was so thankful. Overcome with joy, I surfaced from my inner hiding place and profusely expressed my gratitude using more words than I usually spoke in a week.

"Oh Aunt Martha," I enthused, "thank you so much. It was wonderful; you are so wonderful. I love you; thank you, thank you!" Again, looking puzzled at the intensity of my reaction, she hugged me.

"You are welcome, sweetie. I loved doing it."

After that day, we only visited her family a few more times before they moved out of state.

Dear Girls,

The one holiday we sort of celebrated was Christmas. Even this was done more out of keeping up appearances than for any other reason. Yet in the thirteen years I lived with them only a few events during this holiday stand out in my mind. The first was shortly after I was kidnapped when a friend of Marilyn's handed the boy and me a beautifully gift wrapped box and told us to share. It was filled with delicious Christmas sugar cookies in the shape of bells, trees, and stars.

The second happened years later near Christmas time. I was vacuuming and stopped for a minute to pick up the mail the mailman had just slipped through the slot. To my surprise the letter on top of the pile was addressed to me. Even though I saw my name, the way it was written seemed peculiar. There in the middle of the envelope above our address was Marilyn Sue Hoskins/Grace Ann Neuharth. *Grace Ann Neuharth?* I briefly wondered who that was, but by this time I had ripped opened the envelope and found a document with a check attached.

The document came from an attorney in South Dakota and contained the last will and testament of a person named Neuharth. It said he had left me fifty dollars. Although I was shocked to learn that someone from my past actually knew how to find me, the reality of having that much money to spend momentarily pushed that thought right out of my head.

I had never been given any spending money, and this wealth was mine! All mine! The document said so! Girls, to help you understand just what a huge amount of money this was to me you need to know that in 1959 bread cost twenty cents a loaf, gas was twenty-five cents a gallon, and minimum wage was a dollar an hour. I was suddenly very rich.

Excitedly, I showed the boy my check, and he grabbed the mail, looking for his own envelope. Lo and behold, there it was! He too had received fifty dollars. We jumped up and down with excitement and spent the next few hours making happy plans. Our happiness lasted until James came home.

The moment we showed him our checks and asked him to cash them for us, he got mad. Real mad.

"You do not open any mail that comes into this house; I don't care if it is addressed to you!" he spat through clinched teeth. "The mail that comes here is ours not yours! Do you understand me?" We nodded in dumb acknowledgement.

Then he delivered the death blow to our happy dreams. "Now, about these checks. I will get them cashed, but since you two have never contributed financially to the family, you will be responsible for purchasing all Christmas gifts this year. I will give you each a list of people to buy for. Whatever is left over, you can keep."

After receiving a list of people we hardly knew, David and I shopped as frugally as possible for gifts, always under the watchful eye of James. When we were all finished, we had the grand total of eighty-nine cents to split between us.

I lost my inheritance that day, but I also lost something even more valuable. Hope. Through all the torment and abuse I had held fast to the prayer that God would help my parents find me. It was now clear to me that if someone from my past knew where I was then my parents also knew and didn't care. It didn't matter to them that I had been kidnapped by these people. No one was coming. Despair dropped a dark cloud over my soul. My prayer changed to "God help me survive."

*D*ear *G*irls,

*O*f all the people who went in and out of our lives during those early years, there was only one who may have suspected that something was wrong. Marilyn's uncle, who had been a bachelor all of his life, came from out of state to visit relatives in California. During his stay with us, they told him he could take my bedroom so he could have some privacy, and I would share a bed with Marilyn and James since they had a king-size bed.

"That simply will not do," he said emphatically. "That is not right! I will sleep on the couch if I have to, but I will not force her to give up her room and make her sleep with you guys."

Uncle Hat, as we called him, simply because he always wore a hat, invited David and me to go to the big city closest to us, which happen to be Los Angeles. We were so excited and held our breath until we got permission. Just the idea of getting out of the house was pure pleasure, but he had so much more in store for us. Our first stop out on the town was a huge dime store, where Uncle Hat handed each of us a one dollar bill. He instructed us to look around and find something we really wanted and buy it for ourselves. The boy asked if he could just save his dollar, but Uncle Hat said, "No, you must spend it!"

After we found something we liked and purchased it, he gave us another dollar bill and another and another in store after store all morning long. We were wild with excitement our arms so full of packages that Uncle Hat had to help us carry them. One of my big purchases was a change purse. I finally had money to put in it! At the end of the day David's pants pockets and my new purse were bulging with change.

The spending spree continued for hours before we broke for lunch. On the way to the restaurant, we passed a movie theater. The boy and I had never been to a movie before, and all during lunch we asked if we could go to a movie instead of continuing shopping. Uncle Hat had to think about that for a while. He did not know if we could handle all the violence in the movie. In the end he gave in and took us to see *Gunfight at the OK Corral.*

It had been such a wonderful day; I didn't want to go home. But we had to go home, and Uncle Hat had to leave, and things went back to the way they always were. Whether Uncle Hat really saw everything for what it was I will never know. I do know that for a few magical hours he made me feel like someone actually cared.

---

*D*ear *L*ibby and *R*ylee,

*B*y the time I was a teenager, Marilyn had decided to attend church again. This decision took the form of going to different churches where the visiting evangelist was someone she already knew from her Bible college days. She thought nothing of driving for an hour or more to attend a meeting. If the evangelist happened to be there on Sunday mornings, we went as a family. With a great deal of pride, she introduced her handsome husband and well-behaved children to her old friends. After the service Marilyn always invited them out to dinner and picked up the tab.

This renewed flare up of religious church attendance lasted about a year. I wish I could tell you she changed her life as a result of all these meetings, but it didn't happen. Away from the spotlight of her old friends, she continued to take drugs and go off on screaming tangents declaring I was killing her.

A few noticeable things did come out of all those meetings. First, David and I were allowed to attend a church not very far from our house. The pastor was a neighbor and offered to pick us up if our parents were working. And although Marilyn only attended once or twice a year, James became a regular and was soon a church board member. Churchgoing had the same affect on his actions at home as it did on Marilyn's: none.

Although I don't remember hearing a salvation message at this church, one Friday night a visiting minister preached that the Bible said, "You have to count the cost of serving God." Instead of giving an altar call, she said that everyone should go home, consider the cost, and come back in three days. At that point, they could accept the Lord if they chose.

I was so disappointed. My heart yearned for God, but I knew I couldn't come back in three days. David and I had to be away the whole week with James, who had signed up to be a counselor at church camp. I felt I had lost my one opportunity to become a child of God.

Imagine my surprise when, on the first night of camp, the preacher gave an altar call with no waiting period involved! And he prayed right then and there for anyone who wanted to accept Jesus. After the benediction, the other teens invited me to go to the snack bar for refreshment, but I declined and headed for a secluded place in the woods. Sitting on the ground under a big tree I thought about what I had just heard. I had been too shy to step out at the altar call, but there, hidden from prying eyes, I told God I really wanted to serve him.

To the best of my ability, I prayed the prayer the preacher had prayed a few minutes earlier, asking Jesus to forgive me of my sins. After sincerely repeating all I remembered, I innocently added, "God, if I accidentally left out anything that I am supposed to say, could you please overlook it and save me anyway?" The answer came in a settled peace deep inside. I knew I was a child of God.

After church camp, I hoped that joining the youth group at church would help me learn more about God. I'm not sure what their agenda was, but learning how God could help you in your daily life wasn't it. I recall several lessons on "Does a dog have a soul?" I had never owned a pet and didn't even like animals, so that series was a loss. As were the endless Bible trivia games they were so fond of. How was knowing the names of King David's children going to help me when Marilyn was screaming in my face and James got that look in his eye?

When the call went out for someone to help the teacher in the class for four- and five-year-olds, I jumped at the chance. I have to admit it was more of an escape maneuver than anything else. After the first week of helping with the class, I realized it was just what I needed. I was the teacher's most eager student. In simple terms, she told the wounded little girl inside my teenage body that God loved me. It was such wonderful news, yet I had suspected it all along.

When I heard that God was an ever-present help in the time of need, I knew it to be the truth. Had he not preserved me in the crazy mixed-up world my captors had created for me? The lesson that had the most impact, however, was the one that proclaimed him a deliverer. I pondered this possibility over and over in my mind. I had prayed that my parents would deliver me from this mess. That prayer had changed to "God, please help me survive." But now I was being told God could deliver me. I dared to take a huge leap of faith and began to ask God to deliver me out of that house and away from my kidnappers.

I was too young spiritually to realize that release from bondage is rarely easy or a quick fix. Even as I prayed, demons were gearing up to suck me even further into despair and damage me as much as possible before deliverance came in my last year of high school.

---

*D*ear *G*irls,

*T*o say that there was no noticeable difference in Marilyn's actions as a result of that year of churchgoing is not really the whole picture. The meetings did renew her interest in charity work. It could be that she hoped this would help her get into heaven. At the very least it made her look good. These acts of kindness took many forms, all of which served to complicate my already confusing life and caused me to pray more fervently for deliverance.

One of the good deeds she took on with a passion was to be a babysitting service for those in need. Since she could not babysit herself (no doubt because her nerves were shot), David and I were drafted to do it for her. Our first assignment was a neighborhood couple with three children. They needed a babysitter to fill in the gap in the mornings from when the father left for work and the mother, who worked the night shift, came home. We had to get up an hour and a half earlier each day and walk three blocks in the dark to their house. We went to school after the mother got home. Marilyn also volunteered us to watch six children for four hours three nights a week while their parents attended college classes. She let us know in very holy terms that we were not permitted to accept money, even if offered, for this was a work of charity.

After a while, she began to spread her missions of mercy to neighbors who needed other kinds of assistance. Such was the case of a small boy in the neighborhood whom she felt needed new shoes. She got his size and presented him with a brand-new pair. At the time I had been asking for new shoes for over a month since mine were a size too small. Her reply had been, "We can't afford any right now, make the best of what you have."

Like a woman driven to atone for some secret sin, her missionary zeal escalated until she was bringing strangers home to live with us. Sometimes whole families moved in. I never knew beforehand when she planned to do this, nor did I know how long they would stay. My job was to feed them and see to it that they were happy. Now and then the guests would help out with the chores, but mostly it was my responsibility.

It was one of these guests who found Marilyn the first time she took an overdose of sleeping pills. An ambulance took her to the hospital where they pumped her stomach and released her a few days later. Although some saw the overdose as a suicide attempt, I had serious doubts. As a rule with Marilyn, there was never any room for uncertainty as to what she meant. I had always pictured that when, or if, she really attempted suicide it would be an in-your-face-no-doubt-about-it event. The psychologist who spoke to her after the overdose determined that it was not premeditated but an accident.

I continued to do all the work out of duty, just to appease her and get her out of my face. I hated confrontations. I never said a word, but inside, as I listened to her railings, I was screaming a barrage of questions. *What did I do so wrong that you hate me? Why do you make things so impossible for me? Why do I have to "raise" you people instead of you raising me?* At times I felt I was the adult in the home and they were the spoiled little brats who always wanted their own way. Of course no clue of my anger ever made it to my prematurely old eyes.

No matter what I did, or didn't do, it made no difference. She had, by this time, thoroughly convinced herself that it was my fault that she had mental problems. I simply was not doing those things necessary to make her happy, at least not to her satisfaction.

Another side effect of her year of religious services was that Marilyn embraced humility. The problem was that it was not her humility she wanted to work on, but mine. She began to take special notice of everything I wore. Growing up I had always worn hand-me-downs from Marilyn's friends and the neighbors. They were nice clothes, so I wasn't overly concerned about them. Being a fashion plate had been the least of my worries. But it was now decreed that if I received a compliment on any article of clothing it must be discarded. I was informed that if I wore something someone else liked, it might cause them to envy. Envy was a sin, and I wouldn't want to cause anyone to sin, now would I? My relationship with God began to change. Even though my Sunday school lessons were still reinforcing the love of God, I was getting a warped message of what Christianity was really about.

It seemed to me that Marilyn had sort of a love-hate relationship with the church. She never stayed with one congregation long, but on the other hand she put preachers up on pedestals and even left some of our upbringing to them. For instance, if I got a report card that wasn't what she thought it should be, I would be dropped off at a pastor's house so he could talk to me. When I asked if I could go to the school football game on a Friday night, the answer was, "Ask the pastor." Most of the time he responded, "Your mother says your chores were not done, so the answer is no. You must learn to do your work before you get privileges."

Eventually I was left with the impression that in order to leave the house I had to have pastoral permission. All this unbalanced religion was building a deep resentment in me. I did not understand why the benevolence work had to be piled on top of all my other duties. *Is there no end to what God expects me to do? It's not fair, God! Why? Why?* I railed silently in a fit of mental and physical exhaustion. *Why are nice clothes okay for others but not me? The pastor's wife has nice things and is always getting compliments! Am I so wicked that you have to humble me special?* It took a lot of years for me to straighten out this twisted theology.

*D*ear *G*irls,

*A*dding to my frustration and loneliness was the fact that no one recognized what was going on. Everyone who knew us thought I was blessed to have wonderful parents like Marilyn and James. The consensus was that I should be the happiest girl in the world.

One morning I was running late for school due to my babysitting job. It happened that two other teenage girls who also rode the bus were running late. About that time Marilyn pulled into the driveway and offered to drive the three of us to school. After she dropped us off, they commented, "You sure do have a nice mother!" I said nothing.

That weekend, I answered a knock on the door to find the two girls stopping by for a visit. I was talking to them through the screen when Marilyn came into the room and said I should invite them in and offer them an ice cream bar. I ushered them into the living room then went into the kitchen and opened the freezer. In spite of everything, I was a bit excited about having company my own age. Maybe things would change and I could have friends.

That fleeting pipedream only lasted until I stepped back into the living room and heard Marilyn say, "Well, girls, I certainly hope that you both are better than Marilyn Sue when it comes to cleaning your parent's house." I watched her walk across the room to the television, run her finger across the top, then point it toward the girls so they could see the dust.

"You see how Marilyn Sue cleans?" she continued.

"She knows that she was supposed to dust all of the furniture, but no, she forgot this one!"

The girls nervously took the ice cream bars then politely excused themselves saying, "We really can't stay; thanks for the ice cream," as they hurried toward the door. In a bittersweet way, I was thankful that at least someone knew what I was up against, even though they could not help me.

I learned that most people are not willing to get involved even when they witness abuse. When I was a sophomore in high school, a lady and her two daughters came to visit Marilyn. They were seated in the living room where I was doing my weekly ironing. The lady was bemoaning the fact that she could not afford to buy herself or her girls a dress for Easter and they really wanted one. Overhearing their conversation, I thought to myself, *Join the club*. I had never had a new Easter dress.

All of a sudden, Marilyn jumped out of her chair and said, "Let's go! If you all want Easter dresses, then Easter dresses you shall have!" I couldn't believe my ears! I was going to get an Easter dress! I should have known better, but hope lives eternal. I wasted no time turning off the iron and following them out the door.

When we got to the department store, the lady and her children headed for the full-price section while I was content to shop the clearance rack. It took me quite a while to find a dress that I felt would pass Marilyn's inspection. It couldn't look pretty enough for me to get a compliment, or I would have to give it away.

I found it just in time. All the other dresses were on the counter. I quickly laid my dress on top of the pile. Marilyn, who had been laughing, turned to me. Narrowing her eyes in that look I had come to dread, she said loud enough for everyone to hear, "Go and put that right back where you got it! You have not done one thing in your whole life that makes you worthy enough to deserve an Easter dress."

In the awkward silence that followed, the lady looked away while I took my dress back to the clearance rack, my eyes on the floor, crushed. No one came to my defense. *Worthy?* I wondered exactly what those little girls or woman had done to make themselves more worthy than me. *Wasn't I the one who did all the work that Marilyn should have been doing? Wasn't I the one who supposedly held her life in my hands? How could she say that I had no worth? I was sure people thought I was an evil person. How could I convince them otherwise? Or should I even try?*

Soon after that incident, I felt I would get a chance to have an outsider listen to me and judge for themselves. Once a year in our high school, each student could talk to a counselor to discuss problems at school or home. I had such an appointment coming up. I thought a lot about whether or not I dared trust the school counselor with my deepest darkest secrets. I was feeling dangerously close to a breakdown. It has been said that people may be hurt for a while when the truth comes out, but they will be damaged for a lifetime if it is kept inside. Out of desperation I had made up my mind to share my heart.

The day of the appointment, my mouth was dry with fear. I was so accustomed to not talking about anything I didn't know where I would find the words. I need not have worried. Once inside the counselor's office, I sat down and took a deep breath, but before I got one word out he informed me that Marilyn had been to see him. "Your mother told me she has a real problem with you. You are not helping out enough around the house. Your grades are not what she expects them to be also. I told her in no uncertain terms that she needed to start cracking down on you more. I will be watching you at school to make sure you get those grades up. Dismissed, you can go now."

I was not permitted to either deny or defend the allegations. I had been judged and found guilty. So much for sharing my heart. I was defeated. That was the last time for a very long time I ever felt inclined to confide in anybody.

A year after her first overdose, Marilyn did it again. It may have been an accident. I was of two minds about it. On one level, my whole life was wrapped up in keeping her happy so that I would not be responsible for her death. Going to sleep and never waking up seemed to be a different story. It was as if it was something she willed to do on her own and not because of any failure on my part. I hate to admit this, but there were times I wished she had succeeded.

After getting her stomach pumped, she was transferred to a mental facility to be evaluated. After a week the psychiatrist pronounced her sane and once again sent her home. That's when she really became unhinged.

*D*ear *G*irls,

*B*y the time I was a senior in high school, Marilyn's drug use had reached an intolerable stage, for us as well as for her. It was then that she began adding alcohol to the uppers and downers. Her body responded with a vengeance. She had one kidney removed and was very afraid the other one was shutting down. Yet she would not stop drinking. Once James took her to the hospital, and the doctor refused to treat her because she was drunk. She began drawing Social Security disability and spent most of her day in bed.

The verbal abuse escalated. At times she was incapable of telling me and David apart. The moment I walked in the house after school, she would be hollering, "Marilyn Sue!"

When I'd go into the bedroom and say, "Here I am," she would inform me that Marilyn Sue had not come home from school. Then I would be ordered out of the house to find her and bring her home. I'd try and try to convince her that I was Marilyn Sue, but she rarely bought it. In exasperation I'd leave the room, wait for a bit and reenter to see if she recognized me. If by some chance she did, I'd have to listen to a long screaming lecture about not coming straight home. Day after day it was the same thing: Marilyn screaming, me saying nothing. There were times I thought I might be the crazy one.

Sitting in science class one day, I passed out cold. At the hospital, the doctor did a blood sugar count and discovered my sugar was low, which he said had caused me to faint. His big concern was my sub-normal temperature.

I was released two days later with the diagnosis that I was suffering from mental fatigue. He was right. I was tired. So very tired: spirit, soul, and body. With everything I had to deal with, it took all the precious mental energy I had to just get through a day. A lot of the time I was totally out to lunch, exhausted, preoccupied, and overwhelmed.

It was also a stressful time for David. Both of us took driving lessons in high school, but neither was able to pass the course. For my part the teacher said that I operated in a vacuum and lacked the mental capacity to ever learn to drive. It was a fairly accurate assessment of my state of mind at the time.

In the midst of this insanity, a lady evangelist Marilyn knew came to our church. I was instructed to tell her friend Esther that she wanted to see her. They had several private meetings while she was in town, and after going home the evangelist continued to counsel her on the phone for hours at a time. If the counseling sessions produced results, I didn't see it. I suspect that, since Marilyn refused to take any responsibility for her own life, her counselor had a hard time making her understand I was not her problem.

It is also possible that Esther had no experience working with someone as far into psychosis as Marilyn. Besides her mental illness, there was the drugs and alcohol. You can't reason with folks like this, especially when they are high, and Marilyn was always high. Esther spent hours on end talking to her, but in reality she was talking to the drugs and alcohol, not the real person. That pretty young woman that she knew in Bible college, full of bright dreams to change the world, had disappeared long ago. All that was left was a shell, a drug-wracked shell of misery that no one could reach.

After a few months, Esther realized she couldn't help Marilyn and turned her attention to the rest of the family. One night, she showed up at our house and told both of them that David and I needed to be out of the house until Marilyn's problem could be resolved. Much to my surprise, they agreed. She then invited both of us to stay with her.

David declined because he was already eighteen and had joined the navy reserve to get extra money for college. He was to report for active duty in one month and figured he could stick it out for that long. When she turned to me for my answer, I did exactly what Pharaoh did in the book of Exodus when Moses asked him when he wanted the frogs out of Egypt. His answer defies explanation. This guy was up to his eyeballs with frogs and here the deliverer was asking, "When do you want to be free?" and Pharaoh said, "Tomorrow."

Just like good old Pharaoh, I told Esther that I would come and live with her at the end of the week. This was my last week of school, and I would be graduating in three days.

"I have to finish this out, but I will come immediately following graduation," I explained.

"Marilyn Sue," she said with some urgency in her voice. "I would be more than happy to drive you to school in the morning and pick you up the last three days. I will see to it that you get to your graduation ceremony also; please come now."

Unlike Pharaoh, who just seems stupid, I felt I had a

reasonable cause to postpone my deliverance. While she talked, my mind raced back to another time when I was about ten years old and another deal like this came up.

Our move from the white two-story house took place before David and I had finished the last week of school. For the remaining five days we were to be dropped off every morning at a neighbor's house. She would see us off to school, and someone else promised to pick us up a few minutes after classes dismissed. At least that was the plan.

That first morning, things went fine. After school, we hit a snag. No one came. David and I waited for hours on the schoolhouse grounds for our ride and finally walked to the morning babysitter's house. We rang and rang the bell, but nobody was home. Having nowhere to go and no way to call anyone, we went back to the one familiar place we knew, our old house. Someone had already moved in so, we slipped around to the backyard and sat down underneath the avocado tree to wait. We were prepared to spend the night outside, but as darkness fell James showed up. Not a word was spoken on the trip to the new house. No apology made. The plan was ditched, and we missed the last four days of school.

I could not risk that happening to me again. I had a long way to go before I could trust anyone. So I maintained that I would come right after graduation and spend three more nights with the frogs.

---

*D*ear *G*irls,

*E*sther lived alone in a Los Angeles apartment. When we met, she had been divorced for two years from her wealthy jewelry-store-owner husband. The moment I walked into her place, I could tell it was a woman's domain. Most everything was shades of pink. Her taste was rather sophisticated, and her apartment showed it.

More importantly than how everything looked was the underlying atmosphere. The confusion and fear that permeated the very walls of our house was not present here. For the first time since I had stayed weekends with Grandma, I experienced a sense of peace.

Esther treated me like a special younger friend. Having spent so many hours talking to Marilyn, she understood a bit of what my life had been and tried to fill in some of the holes in my upbringing. At one point she sat me down and told me about the birds and bees using a book that showed various body parts and their functions. All I could think as she talked was, *If you only knew.*

When I moved in, she gave me a beautiful night gown and robe set. It was a full length, silky chiffon, with yellow flowers drifting over its creamy sheerness. I slipped it on and became a princess! I loved the way it flowed and swayed around me as I moved. My nightgowns had always been someone else's castoffs. The tag on this one said it came from Saks Fifth Avenue. It was the first new thing I had received for a very long time, and the idea that someone spent that much money on me was amazing. Maybe I was worth something after all. Esther seemed to think so.

Another marvelous change was having someone else cook. Except for Aunt Martha's Thanksgiving dinner, no one had cooked for me since I was ten years old. Esther's meals were very healthy and served with style. No hot dogs with macaroni here. The food was delicious, and her place settings added the perfect touch. The deep pink band on shining clear crystal matched the rest of her décor. I loved them.

James and Marilyn's dishes were ugly. I'm talking really ugly. We had gotten them free from the Jewell Tea Company, whose trucks came around to houses selling everything from baking powder to cleaning supplies. You buy enough products, you get a dish. The pattern was called Autumn Leaf, and, although I find it hard to believe, they are now highly sought after collectibles. Back when I had to fill them with food, wash them, and put them away every day for seven years straight, I could not appreciate what people now call their "vintage charm."

To further my neglected education, Esther also wanted to teach me to be a hostess. Every night she added a special finishing touch to our dinner plates. From her I learned how to make radish roses and to add a bit of parsley to make everything look festive. All the little niceties that had been absent from my life I found in my new home.

To top off this amazing turn of events, I had money! About a month before I graduated, James had arranged for me to get a job with a parking lot company in L.A. At first, I only worked Saturdays to train, but after moving in with Esther, I was put on full time. My duties included taking care of the switchboard and balancing out the number of tickets turned in with the collected money at the end of the day.

This job boosted my self-image. I was good with numbers, and after getting over my initial shyness and fear of making a mistake, I enjoyed it a lot. I even began to make friends with another girl who worked there. It's hard to explain how excited I was to get my first paychecks. I hadn't had any spending money since Uncle Hat gave us dollars all day long back in 1957, so when I cashed those checks, the first thing I did was go shopping!

I had always had a fascination with sailor dresses, so I bought a sharp-looking one with piping on the collar, a royal blue jumper, a white blouse with a long scarf at the collar that could be tied into a bow or square knot. When I wore my up-to-the-minute outfits with my new white flats with the little strap running across the top of my foot, everyone said I looked cute! I also remember purchasing a black pantsuit and a short-sleeve black top. What was so neat about it was that it had gold and silver threads running up and down all through the fabric. That outfit generated a lot of compliments also. And if I do say so myself, I looked really good!

I was never very adept at fixing my own hair, but I had admired a girl in high school because her hair always looked good and she never wore the same style two weeks in a row. Once I had overheard her say she spent her allowance at the beauty shop. Since it worked for her, I figured it might work for me. Near my job was a beauty college, and I decided to go there instead of going to an expensive salon. I was somewhat frugal with money; maybe some of Grandma's ways had rubbed off on me after all. Every week I let the budding stylist at the beauty school experiment with different hairstyles.

One day, the gals did my hair in an updo that looked very grown up and elegant. So, daring woman of the world that I was, I ventured into a large fancy department store called the May Company and had my picture taken. When I got it back, I was amazed at how beautiful it had turned out. I looked like a model. The portrait studio requested permission to use my photo for promotional purposes. Of course I said yes. So, for several months my picture hung in a fancy building on the corner of Eighth and Hill in downtown Los Angeles.

After moving in with Esther, everything on the surface changed. Away from all the stress, I found life pretty great. It was such a wonderful feeling to wake up in the morning in a pink-hued bedroom, go out to the kitchen to leisurely eat a nice little breakfast, get dressed without someone yelling at me, catch a bus, and go to my very own job and make my very own money and spend it all on just myself.

I reveled in my deliverance. Deliverance was magnificent! Who knew a person could be so happy! It felt so good to be free from the pressures of running a house. Free from the abuse. Free from James. Just free! God had actually delivered me! I had survived, and I had been delivered!

But even as all these wonderful things were happening, other not-so-wonderful things were in the works. Outside things had changed, but inside I was still a prisoner locked in the chains of bondage that had held me all my life. Fear, my old jailer, was standing in the wings waiting to drag me back into the torture chamber.

---

*D*ear *G*irls,

  *O*ne of the not-so-wonderful things brewing included the fact that James kept coming around. After the first few blissful days with Esther, it was apparent that he would be a constant visitor to the pretty little pink apartment. He stopped by every night after work to have dinner with us. They said it was because they both were on the same diet to lose weight. He was his charming enduring self, and Esther seemed to enjoy his company. This was a development that I had not planned on. They were at ease with each other, and I was the uneasy one. I'd eat quickly and disappear into the bedroom.

  I had been living there about a week when dinner was interrupted by the phone ringing. Esther answered and immediately handed the phone to James.

  "Calm down. What's wrong?"

  "Okay, okay, listen, son, you did the right thing. Wait until the pastor gets there. He knows what to do. I'm on my way."

  James hung up and quickly dialed another number.

  "Joe, this is James. Can you get to my house as fast as possible? Marilyn may have committed suicide. My son is there, and by now hopefully our pastor is with him."

  James slammed down the phone, said a few words to Esther, and ran out the door. I had been watching their faces, not fully grasping what was going on. Suddenly, I became aware that Esther was talking to me. "Marilyn Sue, we have to go. Let me get my purse." I stood up and started gathering dishes. "No, no," she interrupted, "leave everything; we can't worry about that now."

We drove the fifty miles in silence, arriving a few minutes after James. The coroner was wheeling out the body as we made our way to the front door. Marilyn had succeeded. This time she did not try pills. David had been in the backyard when he heard the gunshot. He found her on the bed already dead. The gun was in her hand next to her temple. Blood had splattered across the room and was seeping from her wound into the bed covers. Out of reflex David took the gun from her hand.

We stayed long enough for the police to ask about her mental condition. David, James, Pastor, and Esther all testified to the fact that she had problems and that this was not her first attempt. I do not remember being questioned. They then asked about the gun. James admitted it was one of his police revolvers. He had brought it home the night before to be cleaned and then left it on the top shelf of the closet in their bedroom. He had locked his handcuffs in the trigger and assumed it could not be fired. He had been wrong.

After the police left, the four of us spent the night at a local motel. No one wanted to sleep in the house. Pastor stayed behind and disposed of the bed clothes, washed down the walls and made arrangements for the mattress to be taken away.

Early the next day, people began coming to the house to offer their condolences. The suicide seemed to shock everyone. We were really good at keeping family secrets. While James notified relatives, some of the neighbor ladies cleaned the house and did the laundry. A lock had been placed on the bedroom door. The three of us stayed in the house that night, and Esther drove back to L.A. It felt strange being there without the yelling and screaming, but it was still a prison. The walls held the memories.

As usual, when someone dies, relatives came out of the woodwork. David missed the visitation because the cousin who had been our caregiver in the large house insisted on getting into the locked bedroom and going through the closet to see if she could find any clothes she was sure Marilyn wanted her to have.

The day of the funeral I remember only a few people. The cousin/caregiver and Grandma were there, but I'm not sure about Grandpa. He had diabetes really bad, and that might have been about the time his leg was amputated. Marilyn's brother Frank and his wife were definitely there. Frank confronted James, blaming him for the whole thing and accusing him of giving her the drugs. He also blamed him for not putting her in a mental facility, where she could get help. It was not in Grandma's nature to attack anybody because of her Christian stance. I never knew for sure how she felt.

I felt nothing. I knew that people expected me to be the heartbroken child who lost a mother. But I wasn't. She had never been a mother to me, and I had no tears to shed. I did not feel sorry for her or for me. I had waited for years for the other shoe to drop. Death had been threatened so often that I expected it. No surprise. It just seemed like the end of a long nightmare. I did feel sorry for David who had experienced the trauma of finding her, but I had stopped crying years before.

The only thing left for me to get through was the funeral. My one experience at funerals had been a little strange. I was about ten years old when one of Marilyn's uncles died. I didn't even know the guy, but during the service I got the most excruciating pain in my head. I thought it was going to explode. Bear in mind, girls, I never get headaches; I have probably only had two my whole life. Anyway the pain was so bad that I passed out. After I came to, I was fine, and it never happen again.

I sat through this funeral in stoic silence. As I passed the casket for the last time, I was not looking at Marilyn as a daughter, but as a victim staring at her abuser's body.

Back at the house after the interment, the church ladies served refreshments. The members of our church acted like her death was of natural causes, saying nothing except "I'm so sorry." A few family and friends tried to comfort us. One person in particular stands out in my mind; she told me that sometimes people blame themselves for things like this when they shouldn't. Then she nullified her good intention by adding, "But that is just my free advice, and you know free advice is worth exactly what you pay for it, right?" Right.

Then it was over. Or at least that is what I assumed. But Marilyn was not under that mound of flowers; she was still in my head.

---

*D*ear *G*irls,

If I had ever entertained the thought that Marilyn's death would make everything okay, I was sadly mistaken. During the thirteen years I had lived with them a lot of damage had been done to my soul. I had never experienced love, or anything close to it, in that house, so I didn't know how to love. All emotion, especially anger and resentment, always had to be repressed. The truth is you cannot turn your emotions off for any length of time and expect to turn them back on at will. I was almost totally numb inside. The only three emotions I had left were fear, obligation, and guilt. I felt totally responsible for Marilyn's death.

Immediately after the funeral the nightmares began. I dreamed Marilyn was standing beside her casket screaming at me, *Marilyn Sue! Why did you let them bury me when I wasn't dead? Wasn't dead! Wasn't dead!*

In the dream I could hear her venom-filled words coming at me, but just like when she was alive I was powerless to speak. Cold sweat soaked my body as I tried to search for an answer that would appease her. At the same time I knew there was none. There never had been an answer she would accept. I was guilty, guilty, guilty. I woke up shaking with terror. It had been so real. She had escaped death to come back and haunt me.

The only scripture I could think of was, "For God hath not given unto me a spirit of fear but of power and of love and a sound mind." I repeated it over and over until the image of Marilyn was erased from my mind and I could go back to sleep.

The nightmares continued at regular intervals for more than seven months. It was always the same: the casket, her angry face, the screaming accusation, and me being struck dumb with guilt and finally awakened to desperately quote the same scripture until she went away. Then I remembered the city of refuge.

The long-past Sunday school lesson at Grandma's church surfaced like a lifeline. With the simple faith of a child, I grabbed it and held on. In my mind the city of refuge became a place for me to park my guilt about Marilyn's death until a determination could be made as to my innocence or guilt. The nightmares ceased. I stayed in that place of safety, not knowing if I was guilty or innocent for another twenty-seven years.

That's when I met a Christian psychologist who convinced me, after many tries, that if a person takes their own life it is because of something inside of them, and I had no part in her decision. That settled it for me. In the court of my mind I had been found not guilty. I hadn't caused her death. It wasn't my fault. At last, I knew I was innocent.

*D*ear *G*irls,

After the funeral, I went home with Esther, and David reported for duty. He was stationed nearby waiting for his final orders. Although I still thought of him as James and Marilyn's son we had developed a special friendship. We talked on the phone often about what he was doing, and I told him about the people at my work. He took a particular interest in Helen, one of my new friends. One day he asked if I would set him up on a blind date with her. I agreed to try. It took a few weeks to talk her into it but she finally agreed. When I told him she said, "Yes," he was like a little boy with a ticket to the circus. It was his first date.

When he came down from his excited high, it dawned on him that he had a couple of problems. Number one, he didn't have a car. Number two, he didn't have a driver's license either. Never at a loss to work an angle the same boy who figured out how to get me to walk home from school while he pocketed my bus fare, quickly solved both problems by planning to rent a car and inviting a buddy along who did have a license. To sweeten the deal, David promised his friend he would pay for everything and get him a date. I was to be the date.

David assured me that Harold was really nice. They had met on base when both were assigned to pick up trash along the highway. David admitted that he liked Harold because he made him laugh. Up until that time there hadn't been much to laugh about in our lives, and Harold's humor helped him get his mind off our weird life.

With his final boyish declaration of "You will really

like Harold, Sis; he's a great guy!" I folded. That clever, fast-talking boy had convinced me to go on a double blind date with him and his friend.

Now I had a problem. I had never been allowed to date or have any contact with the opposite sex. I had no idea how to act around a boy. I was just learning how to act around people in general, and the thought of a date was more than a little unsettling. *What do you talk about to a boy? And what to wear! My goodness what will I wear?* Going through all my new clothes, I finally decided on the royal blue jumper, white blouse, and white shoes. When my date showed up, he seemed to like what he saw, telling me I looked pretty. I was less impressed with him.

Harold wasn't bad looking, at about five feet nine with sandy blond hair and blue eyes, but definitely not what I expected. He was loud and a little on the rough side. I was hoping for someone a little gentler. He also smoked and seemed to be the nervous sort. My experience with nervous folks was not something I was anxious to repeat. His one redeeming quality was he could make you laugh.

We went to an amusement park for the better part of the day and rode every ride available. Afterwards we ate at a Chinese restaurant where Harold kept up a running comment on everything. Evidently they didn't have Oriental food where he came from because he spent the whole meal asking what he was eating. When he asked the waiter, "So what do we use these little shovel-type spoons for?" we lost it.

At the end of the evening, we took David's date home first. Back at Esther's, the guys walked me to the door and waited while I searched for the key in my purse. When I couldn't find it, I rang the bell and called, "Esther, I forgot my key! Open the door!"

"Oh, okay, just wait a minute."

While we waited, Harold talked to David. I didn't pay much attention until I heard him say, "You know what, buddy? I'm going to marry your sister someday."

That announcement came as a complete surprise for me. In my opinion the boy was getting way ahead of himself. *Marry him?* That did not seem to be in the realm of my possibilities. I may not have known what my type was, but I was pretty sure he wasn't it. I wasn't even certain I wanted to date him again. As I closed the door behind me, I was saying to myself, *I don't think so.*

Glad it was over, I crawled into bed. As I laid my head on my pillow, the room began to spin. I figured the day of wild carnival rides had made me lightheaded. The truth was not so simple. As usual, my subconscious knew something my head didn't know. History was about to repeat itself. I had no idea I had just gotten on another kind of wild ride and it would be a long, long time before I could get off again. I had just had my first date with your grandfather.

---

*D*ear *G*irls,

The morning after the date, the phone rang very early. I could not think who would call me at six a.m., but it was David.

"Sis, I've just received my orders. I pulled overseas duty and leave tomorrow for Japan. I guess I won't be seeing you for the next three years. Sorry I couldn't tell you in person, but that is the way it goes in the military. Write to me often."

"Oh no! I'm going to miss you! I wish you could have been stationed stateside."

"I know, me too, but at least Harold will still be here. This is homeport for his ship. The two of you really should get together. He can keep you company while I'm gone. Well, got to go, there are others waiting for the phone...bye." And he was gone. The thought of David leaving the country made me very sad. No day of my remembered life had been without him.

I really did not want to go out with Harold again, but for David's sake I figured I could date him a few more times and see how things went. I didn't have much free time anyway. My job took up my daytime hours, and I had signed up for a speed writing class in the evenings. Most nights I would not come home for dinner. It was quicker to just grab a bite to eat after work so I could make it to my night class on time.

Not only did I not have much dating time, this schedule worked well for me because it meant less time to spend around James on his continued visits to the apartment. I had been so busy with my new life that I failed to notice what was going on right under my nose. I was stunned when Esther sat me down one day and told me they were going to be married.

"Now, I know, dear, that this happened all of a sudden. It has only been four months since your mother died, but your father and I really love each other and want to be married in a few weeks. I would love to have you continue living with us after we get back from the honeymoon. What do you say?"

I didn't know what to say. My thoughts raced. *How terrible! Dare I try to talk her out of it? What should I do?* Yet my experience with adults had convinced me that when they make up their minds to do something nothing I said or thought mattered. I was also scared. I wasn't at all sure what would happen if I told her about James. *Would she believe me or get mad and kick me out on the street? And what about him? Would he seek revenge?*

If there was one thing I was well versed in, it was the conspiracy of silence. I came from a long line of secret keepers. It was in my physical and emotional DNA. Secrets were our tradition, our family business, so to speak. Getting out of the secret keeping business was something I was unable to do at that point. I did not try to dissuade her. I did not tell her what kind of man he really was. I did not tell her how he had abused and terrorized me all those years. I kept my mouth shut and lived to regret it.

The one thing I was able to do was make the decision not to live with them and possibly go back into the same situation with him again. That I could not do. To think about living under the same roof with James filled me with unspeakable dread. When I found my voice, I answered in the politely pleasant way secret keepers do. "Thanks for the invitation to live with you guys. I know I'm welcome, but it is about time for me to start my life and get a place of my own."

Girls, if I could go back, I would have blown the whistle on James then and there. I wanted to do the right thing, but I was in a state of paralysis due to the fear of death or abandonment. I also lived in denial. Denial is a lie you tell yourself, and I had used it for years as a defense mechanism to make the pain go away. Lie to yourself long enough, and you set a stage to deceive others.

I actually convinced myself that he would not abuse anyone else, thinking I was his only victim and he only came to me because Marilyn didn't meet his needs. Yes, I know now this is warped thinking, but most child molesters teach their victims how to think. In some situations victims are fully convinced by the abuser that it is their own fault or they are doing the abuser a great service.

The dynamics between a molester and his victim can go on and on for years. You can be thousands of miles away from your abuser, and he can control your mind, keeping you as deep in bondage as if you lived in the same house. The prison is inside us. A victim gets free when her soul gets free. I was nowhere near free.

The truth about molesters and pedophiles has been a long time coming, and it took even longer for the general public to face the truth. Years ago, I read a nationally syndicated advice column where a teenage girl wrote in and said her uncle was a child molester. That uncle and her aunt were going to Florida and had invited her. She asked for advice as to whether or not it would be safe for her to go. The columnist said, "Go, you will be okay." A few days later the columnist wrote an apology saying she had received so many letters from all across the country explaining abuse to her and telling her she gave this girl bad advice. The columnist went on to say she broke one of her rules and personally called the girl and told her she was wrong and the girl shouldn't go.

These days a wealth of information is readily available about this widespread epidemic. That was not the case the first fifty or so years of my life. Since then I have learned a few things. For one, I discovered that James perfectly fit the profile of many child abusers. They are generally popular with both children and adults, appear to be trustworthy and respectable, have a good standing in the community, are usually family men, have no criminal record, and deny that they abuse children. It does not occur to a molester that he is destroying a child's life.

Pedophiles will go to great lengths to gain access to their young victims. Like James, many volunteer for church youth groups, as camp counselors, and as coaches for kid's athletic teams. They are also master manipulators and use guilt, fear, and even love to confuse the child and buy their silence. Children who are lonely, emotionally unstable, from broken or abusive homes are prime targets. Experts say that a single molester can abuse one hundred to four hundred children in his lifetime if he is not stopped.

Stopping him is easier said than done. For years, the

church dropped the ball on understanding molesters and pedophiles. One mother walked in on her husband molesting her nine-year-old daughter and went to her pastor. The misinformed pastor assured her that once an abuser is caught he will never do it again. The mother believed him, and the child endured the abuse for another nine years. Today, she is a wounded, bitter woman passing on her anger to her own children. She hates her mother and her mother hates herself.

Unfortunately, religious thinking has also served to propagate these atrocities. In my own case, I knew that Esther was a woman of God, an evangelist who knew God and could hear his voice. She prayed and read her Bible. My thinking was that if she needed to know all that stuff about James surely God could tell her. What I didn't understand is just because a person can hear from God in one area does not mean he can get through to them in all areas. When a woman has convinced herself that she is in love with Mr. Right, even God has a hard time getting her to see clearly.

Another area that has tripped up too many Christians is unclear teaching on forgiveness. The victim is told, "God has forgiven the abuser, so why do you still want to talk about it?" Well, we need to talk about it because 95 percent of the forgiven pedophiles go back to their old tricks if they do not get godly counseling and supervision over a prolonged period of time.

Not that God didn't truly forgive them; in many cases the repentance is sincere and forgiveness real, but unless the person owns his problem and figures out what wound in his soul causes him to do such terrible things, he is a danger to children. He may hate himself and even quit for a while with every intention of changing his life, but the demons keep calling his name, and sooner or later another child's innocence is ripped from her.

Even if the victim forgives them, too many Christians get confused about the next step. Lewis B. Smedes states in *The Art of Forgiving*, "When you give up vengeance, make sure you are not giving up on justice... Vengeance is personal satisfaction; justice is moral accounting. Human forgiveness does not do away with human justice."

My dear granddaughters, how I wish I had known these things when I sat on the couch with sweet Esther those many years ago. I looked at her happy shining eyes and saw a woman dreamily in love with a man who could be charming and likeable. I really wanted to believe that this new beginning would make a new man out of him. I really wanted to believe that Marilyn had caused all of our problems and now all of us could be happy. I was delusional. In later years, I heard about his ongoing inappropriate behavior with the little girls in their church. When you keep secrets about abuse, you never know how many lives it affects down the road.

I wish with all my heart that this letter could be handed to all the precious little girls James may have abused since then. I long to say to each and every one of them, "I am so sorry. I didn't know; please forgive me. I didn't know what to do. I wanted to do the Christian thing, but I messed up. I was afraid. Secrets were all I knew. I had no inner resources to make wise judgments. I didn't understand the danger I would be placing you in. I am so very sorry."

How I wish every single child who has been scarred by a pedophile or a molester could hear a heartfelt apology from the people who should have protected them and didn't. "Please know it was not your fault. It was not your fault. Please forgive us and please do not make the same mistake we did. Tell someone."

*D*ear *G*irls,

*T*he weeks after I learned of James and Esther's intention to be married were stressful. James was around all the time, and Esther continued to glow. They were persistent in inviting me to live with them after the wedding, and Harold kept calling asking me for dates. I said no to them and yes to Harold a few times. When he'd picked me up at the apartment, James was always there to welcome him. The two good old boys really liked each other. More than once, on our way out the door, James threw Harold his car keys so we wouldn't have to ride a bus. Of course Harold thought James was great. That should have told me something.

I moved out before the wedding. Esther finally accepted my decision to leave and helped me find a place to live. It was in a dorm-turned-hotel facility and owned by a Christian organization. Each tiny room contained a twin bed, a desk, a chair, a dresser. The sink stood in the corner, and the bathroom was down the hall. The building was split into two sections with males on one side and females on the other. A church/college facility separated them. The house rule of no visitors of the opposite sex allowed in your room was strictly enforced. That suited me fine. I felt safe. My new address was on South Hope Street in the City of the Angels. Seemed like a perfect place to start my new life.

In retrospect, it seems as if God really had set me up in an ideal situation. Not only could I walk to work, there were a number of restaurants in the area and a coffee shop on the corner. Although I was now truly on my own, I did not have to worry about running out of money. The parking lot company where I worked had a policy that if you are ran short in any given week all you had to do was to tell your supervisor how much you needed, sign a form and you got an advance.

My first visitor after moving in was Harold. He called on the house phone, and I suggested we meet at the corner coffee shop. Over hamburgers and fries, I told him about David's latest letter.

"He's getting settled in the Japanese port. Oh, and guess what? His ship is small, and they don't have a chaplain aboard, so the captain asked if anyone wanted to volunteer to fill in as chaplain to let him know, so he volunteered. He is now chaplain aboard the ship and will do the Sunday worship services. Not too bad for a nineteen-year-old!" I finished proudly.

"Marilyn, that's wonderful! You know I've always liked your brother from the first time I met him. He always seemed depressed, though, so I tried to cheer him up. After a while, he opened up and told me all about how your father had killed your mother."

I looked at him blankly as my mind raced back to the day Marilyn died. *Why would David say James was responsible for her death? That couldn't be. He was at Esther's apartment when it happened. It was an accident that he had left his gun on the bedroom shelf. Wasn't it? Hadn't he clipped his handcuffs in the trigger to prevent it from firing? What on earth? Did David really think James killed her and why would he tell a total stranger something like that anyway?*

Harold noticed my mind had drifted off somewhere so

he paused until he thought that I was listening again then rattled on, "To just slit her throat like that and then kill himself was awful. It helped me understand why he was so down on life. This thing with your adoptive mother shooting herself brought back all those memories. Seeing another dead body in a pool of blood would cause anybody trauma."

I slowly lowered my half-eaten hamburger to the plate. Staring at Harold with wide eyes, I listened closer. *What was he saying? I had no idea what he was referring to. Who slit whose throat then killed himself? Was he nuts? Why else would he blurt out such a wild story and assume I knew what he was talking about?*

He must have read something in my face, because he asked, "You did know that, didn't you? I mean, you seem so surprised."

I thought the whole conversation was ridiculous, and deep inside I was getting aggravated. I didn't have a clue what he was talking about, but I knew I wanted to change the subject, so I lied and flippantly answered, "Sure, I knew it. You just caught me off guard. Now, can we talk about something else?" We never discussed it again.

*D*ear *G*irls,

*A*fter I blew off Harold's announcement that my father had slit my mother's throat and changed the subject, our date preceded without a glitch, until I asked out of curiosity, "So, why do you smoke?" His answer sealed my fate.

"I smoke because my nerves are shot."

At that moment, I knew I would marry him. His words flashed me back to the thousands of times Marilyn had said her nerves were shot and it was up to me to keep her from committing suicide. Before I could shake the thought, my mind presented a possibility that here was a second chance to make up for her death. Maybe I could keep Harold from the same consequence by not disappointing him in what he expected me to do.

James and Marilyn had raised a highly developed people pleaser who was delusional enough to think she was responsible for everyone who crossed her path. So I resigned myself to fulfilling Harold's first date prophecy of our marriage. It was now my duty to make him happy.

Harold was nice to me, and he helped fill my weekends. I was beginning to like him. We would have many more dates before he had to leave for seven months sea duty. It was decided that we would be married when he returned. After he left, I had more than a few second thoughts about him and ample time to ponder my fate.

I actually did not want to get married. My take on the world had come from living with my captors, so my only perception of married life was through their eyes and that was not a pretty picture. *Besides,* I asked myself, *since I am only eighteen and have never had a life of my own, did I really want to marry the only guy I ever dated?* I didn't think so. My resolve lasted until Harold threatened me.

At first I tried to slow down my letters in hopes he would get tired and break it off. It only made him mad. Really mad. He informed me that if I didn't start writing regularly letting him know what I was doing he would go AWOL and come see for himself. Having no experience at standing up to anybody, I buckled and did what he expected me to do. That act was a preview to our marriage.

But, and it was a big but, until he came home, I was game for a little excitement, and I had a new friend at work who knew where to find it. Babs was a year older than me, owned a two-passenger sports car, and knew her way around. I liked her even though I suspected she was a tad bit wild. Of course, compared to me, the little old ladies down at the bingo parlor were wild.

Babs knew how to have a good time, and, like David, I could use a few laughs. Often after work, we'd hop in her car and drive to one of the hot spots in Pasadena. Her favorite was a small place located in an old ice warehouse that you entered through an alley. In the 1960s, when folk music was in its prime, the Ice House was America's top folk and comedy club. Comedians and music groups came from all over the country to perform. I remember some great groups such as The Shaggy Gorillas Minus One Buffalo Fish and The Irish Rovers, who recorded "Grandma Got Run Over by a Reindeer." I know you girls are laughing right now, but I did not make up these names.

One night at the Ice House, a couple of guys from the

band began flirting with Babs, and she was giving back as good as she got. After the show they asked us if we wanted to go grab a bite to eat, so we followed them to a restaurant in her car. Although Babs and I were, theoretically "all grown up" at ages eighteen and nineteen, that night, we didn't feel the need to impress anyone with our maturity. After ordering our food we began laughing and cutting up like a couple of fifteen-year-olds.

At the next table, a very proper young lady about our age clearly did not appreciate our hilarity. I heard someone call her name and realized we may have gone to high school together. Of course, she would have never connected the mousy, walking-with-her-head-down Marilyn Sue to the cute wild child giggling at the next table.

Finally, turning around and looking at us with raised eyebrows, she said, "Why don't you two act your age and quiet down!" Naturally, that set us off again. That night everything was hilarious. It was a fun evening, but after dinner we said good-bye to the band boys and went home. The next time we went to the Ice House we almost got arrested.

Our close encounter with the law took place the night we met a guy at the club who claimed to be the Surfing King of Malibu. We talked a while, and sometime after midnight, the king invited us both over to his parent's house for a snack. As he led us into the kitchen to get soft drinks, he whispered for us to keep it down because his folks were asleep.

Suddenly, his father came down the stairs in his pajamas, looking scared and none too happy to see us. Turning to the Surfing King of Malibu, he demanded, "Just what do you think you are doing sneaking in here at this hour?" Before the king could answer, Papa said, "I thought you were a burglar and called the police. They will be here any minute! You all better leave before they come or you will have a lot of explaining to do!"

Needless to say, that little car lost no time getting on down the road.

---

*D*ear *G*irls,

*W*ild or not, some of Babs' free-spirited ways must have rubbed off on me. One day I got the notion in my head to go to a city I had never been to and see if I could survive a weekend without anyone's help. Of course the plan had a few holes in it, but, after all, I was making decisions on my own for the first time. This consider-all-the-angles business was new to me. I had lived my entire life under a banner that read "No Thinking Allowed," so, in this wonderful-unaccustomed-freedom-of-choice world I now found myself in, it never occurred to me that Labor Day weekend might not be the best time to prove a point. Nor did I figure out what I would do if I should discover I couldn't survive without help. Whom would I turn to? The thought of calling up James and saying, "Hey, Dad, I'm four hundred miles away and got a little problem," was so out of the question it was ludicrous.

Although I didn't have a lot of money, in fact, I doubted I'd have enough to make it back home, I wasn't worried. I figured if I ran out all I would have to do is go to the nearest parking lot owned by the company I worked for and ask for a payday advance. I already knew there were plenty of them in the city I wanted to visit.

I hatched this magnificent scheme on Saturday morning, and by noon I was on a bus to the airport. I did not pack any clothes or tell anyone where I was going. I just went. I was my own woman, and I would sink or swim on my own. I bought a one-way ticket to San Francisco,

California; paid for it in cash; and was handed an envelope in return.

I was feeling cocky and on-top-of-my-game that when a cute sailor tried to pick me up in the airport I flirted back. In an easy laid-back drawl, he asked me where I was going. When I answered, he gave me an engaging smile and declared, "Well, I'm from Texas, and I got me a flight back home right now or else I might just be tempted to change my plane and go to San-fraan-ciss-co." I humored him along for ten minutes or so until my flight was announced, flashed him a grin, and said, "Well, bye now, gotta go," and took off for my gate.

My new persona proceeded up the ramp without the least bit of nervousness at getting on an airplane for the first time. I had survived scarier things than flying to a strange city alone with little money. I boarded the plane with what I hoped was a sophisticated air of knowing, found a seat, and buckled up. Settling back in the seat, I was ready for my adventure.

After all the preliminaries had taken place and we were well on our way, the stewardess came along to collect our tickets. As she approached me she said, "Well, I can see that this is your first flight. How are you enjoying it?"

"How do you know this is my first flight?" I inquired, wanting to know what gave me away. I had tried my best to look like a seasoned traveler as I efficiently handed her my envelope.

"Why, you're the only one still wearing a seatbelt. Everyone else took theirs off when the overhead sign came on. So, where is your ticket?"

"I just handed you my ticket; it's in that envelope," I answered, a little peeved that she had seen through my seasoned traveler ruse.

"There is nothing in here. It's empty. Where did you purchase the ticket?"

"At the airport just before flight time," I answered, feeling a bit less confident.

"I'll call the airport and see if they have a record of you purchasing a ticket."

I nervously waited while she finished her rounds and made the call. She finally returned to inform me that the airport staffer had failed to include my ticket in the packet. I took a deep breath. Okay, first hurdle jumped. I was going to be all right.

It was late afternoon when we landed in San Francisco. I caught an airport shuttle to historic downtown Union Square. The streets were full of tourists like me just taking in the sights. I wandered in and out of shops until my stomach began to growl, then I looked around for a place to eat. A couple nearby was talking about restaurants and when I overheard the lady say, "Let's eat at Foster's tonight" I thought, *Sounds good to me,* and nonchalantly followed them down the street to the famous restaurant.

The sun was setting by the time I had finished my delicious meal and began to think about where I would spend the night. On my walk around the square, I had located at least four hotels. Backtracking, I inquired at each one about the availability of a room. The answer was the same, "It's Labor Day, lady; we are booked solid." At the last hotel, the desk clerk must have seen the concern in my face and asked me to wait a minute while he called a couple of places.

I was contemplating the possibility of spending the night on a park bench when he said, "I found a hotel with one room left. They can hold it just five minutes for you. It is one block up and two blocks to the right. You better get going, or you'll miss it."

I thanked him, sprinted for the door, and made it just in time. At the new hotel, the clerk handed me the key to the last empty room in the building and possibly the whole city. He explained I could only have it for one night, as it was rented for the rest of the weekend. Up in my room, I closed the door, locked it, and gleefully threw myself across the bed, grinning from ear to ear. I had done it! I had boarded a plane and flown to San Francisco, California, all by myself! Now here, I was well fed, safe and sound in my very own hotel room. After hanging up my dress, I stretched out in the unaccustomed luxury of a full-sized bed. I was mightily impressed with myself and thankful to God. Everything had worked out so perfectly, and I still had a full day ahead. I soon drifted into a deep, happy, dreamless sleep.

The next morning, I asked for directions to the one place I really wanted to see, Fisherman's Wharf. I was told to catch the next trolley. Still in my I-can-do-this mode, I stood at the stop with a group of other people and patiently waited until the trolley came. I soon discovered that San Francisco trolleys were not L.A. buses. No orderly, single file lines here. When the trolley slowed, the people around me suddenly turned into an out-of-control mob pushing, shoving, and grabbing for anything that would help them get on board. In a matter of seconds they were gone, and I stood on the sidewalk watching the trolley roll down the street wondering, *What just happened?*

Well now! Hmmm! As others gathered around to wait for the next trolley, I made a few adjustments in my thinking. I decided when another one showed up, there would be no more missy nice gal. I figured I could grab and hang on with the best of them. I was determined. As the trolley slowed down and the horde moved forward, I pushed, shoved, grabbed, held tight, and swung on. *Okay! Done!*

Flushed with success, I triumphantly paid my fare, found a seat and re-gathered my dignity by smoothing the wrinkles out of my dress. *Yes, I could do this!* After twenty minutes the conductor yelled, "End of the line!" I got off and found myself in Golden Gate Park. Oh well, it was nice, and I enjoyed the beautiful flowers, but this was not where I wanted to go. The next time I caught a bus that took me to my real destination.

Fisherman's Wharf was all I expected and more. All the sights, sounds, and scents I had read about were there in living, breathing, beautiful color. The water was deep azure blue, the sky a few shades lighter, gulls noisily dipped and dived flashing white wings in the morning sun. The sea roared with each wave that surged toward the shore.

Out in the middle of the bay, I could see Alcatraz Island and the infamous prison fortress, which had recently been closed. Some years after this visit they turned the fortress into a museum. Years later when I visited the prison, I saw, in one of the rooms, a list of prison rules and regulations. In 1934 rule number 5 was: "You are entitled to food, clothing, shelter, and medical attention. Anything else you get is a privilege." When I read that it struck me that I had lived with Alcatraz Rule No. 5 most of my life.

But on this day, I was no longer in my captor's power. I was free. I walked the piers breathing the salty air and watched the fishing boats. After a while I sat down at an outdoor cafe overlooking the bay and ate my way through a pile of shrimp served with freshly made sourdough bread slathered with real butter. Below my table, near the water, an old fisherman was mending his net. I smiled to myself and to the world, freedom felt good.

I had originally planned to spend the whole weekend in San Francisco, but after last night's experience finding a hotel, I decided to go home. In the late afternoon as the foghorns moaned in the bay, I caught a shuttle for the airport and bought a ticket home. This time, seasoned traveler that I was, I checked the envelope to see if the ticket was indeed inside. As I boarded the plane, I felt as if I had just taken on Mount Everest and made the summit. Yes, I could survive alone.

Got to tell you, girls, my impetuous decision to take this adventure did wonders for my self-esteem. I came back feeling empowered to take on the rest of my life.

---

*D*ear *G*irls,

*A*fter I moved out, I did not see much of Esther. She had to leave the pretty pink apartment when the landlord found out she was dating James and no longer holding evangelistic meetings. He had rented it to her at a really good price because she was doing the Lord's work. They moved twenty miles away to a smaller town where she owned an apartment complex that was a part of her divorce settlement. I saw James from time to time when he stopped by my work place. He and my boss were buddies.

Soon after I returned from San Francisco, my hours changed to where I was working from four in the afternoon to midnight. I didn't mind working nights too much since I had little else to do except shop and write letters to Harold and David. Babs had the same hours, and we still made late-night runs up to Pasadena when we got off work.

The only drawback of this new shift was even on my days off I was still wide eyed at midnight. One Sunday evening I got restless and decided to go for a walk. I strolled for a few blocks stopping here and there to peer into store windows. Suddenly someone walked up behind me and said, "You look like an angel staring in that window." Taken aback, I turned to face a nicely dressed man about thirty years old. I moved on, and he followed.

It soon became apparent he was trying to pick me up. Although I was a tag along on my friends' flirting sprees with the boys at the club and had enjoyed the ten-minute exchange with the young sailor at the airport, I had not dated anyone other than Harold and knew nothing about men. This guy was making me uncomfortable, and I wasn't sure how to get rid of him.

As I turned back toward the hotel, he walked alongside talking about his beach house and offering to take me there. He said he just wanted to walk on the beach and talk for a while. I mumbled, "No, thank you. I'm engaged to be married." As I hurried on, he dropped back, and I wasn't sure if he was following or not. Ducking into the hotel lobby, I rushed to the elevator and was soon safe in my room on the fourth floor. Getting ready for bed, I tried to shake it off, thinking, *What a strange man*. I was glad it was over.

It wasn't near over. The next morning, the phone rang early. He asked me where my fiancé was and if I was sure that I didn't want to go out with him. He said he was well to do and could give me whatever I wanted. I answered, "No, thank you," and slammed down the receiver. How had he known my name? He would have to have it to have a call transferred from downstairs to my room. It was unsettling to say the least.

He knew more than my name. The calls came like clockwork, every night and every morning, day after day, night after night. He wanted to know why I didn't have an engagement ring and when my fiancé would get home from sea duty. With each fact he revealed, I became more frightened. Where was he getting the personal information? Who would tell him about Harold? Besides Babs, James, and Esther, no one knew anything about my personal life.

When he called, I always hung up quickly, praying he would go away, but nothing deterred him. Like most stalkers, he had an agenda all his own and would not heed the word *no*. As the days flowed into weeks, fear and paranoia became my constant companion, and my world again filled with impending doom. At times I felt I was literally going crazy. The simple act of walking down the street sent me into a frenzy of worry. I was sure I was being followed, but when I looked back no one was there. My fevered mind imagined he had ducked into a shadow or a doorway. I stopped going out alone if I could help it.

Eventually I spent all my spare time in the tiny hotel room alone staring at the phone, willing it not to ring. When it did ring I wouldn't answer. Fear and freedom cannot coexist, and the lovely freedom I had so relished was a thing of the past.

The girl with the growing self-esteem who shopped for cute clothes, got her hair done, flew to San Francisco alone, flirted with a sailor, went to a comedy club, and enjoyed a fit of giggles in a restaurant had disappeared. The old Marilyn Sue had returned, and she had nothing in common with the fun-loving, brave, excited-about-life girl she almost became. I once again walked in fear with my head down waiting for the next catastrophe to hit.

The stalker experience brought back all the old feelings of being abused, except it was worse. Unlike my years with James and Marilyn, which was a more controlled abuse and had become part of a routine I expected, the stalker's abuse was an outside force, and I never knew when he would strike or what he would do. I didn't know if he was a harmless nut or an ax murderer.

For a while, I felt a degree of safety while at work. Then one by one my coworkers stopped by my office telling me a man answering the description of the stalker had been visiting the various parking lots asking for information about me. Some of the parking lot guys were concerned about my safety and warned me, "Be careful, Marilyn. This man is crazy and dangerous; don't take any chances. We told him your father was a cop, so he better not mess with you if he knew what was good for him!" These reports added a new level of alarm to my growing terror. If even guys at work were afraid of him what chance did I have? Strangely, their threats of my cop father didn't faze him in the least.

One night after work it was unusually overcast, even for L.A. Babs always dropped me off directly in front of my door, but tonight when we got to the corner nearest the hotel, the street had been blocked off. We could faintly see a group of people at the other end of the block near the library where the street dead ended. I wondered who they were. L.A. had recently gone through the Watts riots, and any group was suspicious.

With apprehension, I got out of the car and began walking as quickly as possible toward my building. In my fear-seized mind, every shadow held danger. I remembered an incident before Harold left when a guy at the hotel had warned us to be careful because a man had been knifed nearby.

Suddenly, a car sped past on the wrong side of the street, slammed on its breaks, and stopped a few feet behind me. Leaving the motor running, the driver jumped out and came after me. I screamed in sheer panic and ran. Behind me my assailant's feet pounded the pavement as he drew closer and closer.

Gasping for breath, I was in a full flight of terror when the street was suddenly flooded with bright lights and behind me someone yelled, "Cut! Cut! Come on, lady! You're right in the middle of our set! Okay, everybody, take it from the top! Cameras ready!"

I had walked into the filming of a Perry Mason episode. The guy who jumped out of the car and chased me was the actor who played Paul Drake.

I should have gotten a good laugh out of this, but it was far too real to be funny. I now knew how vulnerable I was to the stalker. He could grab me off the street any time he wanted to. I was at his mercy. But what could I do?

I had no one to turn to. To take Esther and James up on their standing invitation to live with them was unthinkable. I knew that if Harold were here I'd marry him in a minute just to have someone to take care of me. I was desperate. The very breath I breathed became a prayer. "God, please help me get out of this alive."

---

*D*ear *G*irls,

*J*ames said he found out about the stalker from someone at work. He was all sympathy, and although he did not offer to have his police buddies watch out for the guy, he did suggest I move and offered to find me a place. Of course I couldn't say no. Insecurity was again paralyzing me, and my faith that I could take care of myself was dwindling by the minute. I needed help even if it was from someone I feared and distrusted.

The place he found was a studio apartment behind Central Receiving Hospital. It had a large living room and a walk-in closet. Inside the closet was a Murphy bed. One wall in the living room was made out of rocks. In its small eat-in kitchen, I could prepare my own meals. It also had a private bathroom, which was a welcome change from having to go to the end of the hall for the public restroom. It was exciting to get a new place. I checked out of the hotel, leaving no forwarding address, confident I had escaped the stalker.

I moved in on a Saturday afternoon with Esther and James's help. They brought some stuff for me from our old home. Because I now had a kitchen, I asked Esther if she had any extra dishes I could use. Guess which dishes she rounded up? Those ugly Jewel Tea dishes that I hated! They had been in storage since Marilyn's death, and now they were all mine. Just lovely! But, as she was carrying them into the apartment, the box slipped from her hands, and every one of those hideous dishes broke into tiny pieces! Under my breath I yelled, *Hurrah!*

We were moving in the last of the boxes when the

landlord stopped by with a message. "Your boyfriend came by yesterday and left his phone number. He wants you to call him if you would like to go out to a movie tonight." Sick to my stomach, I wadded the piece of paper and threw it away. With a sinking heart, I realized it had not worked. How could he have possibly found me even before I moved in? Who told him where I was? No one knew my address except Esther and James.

I felt more vulnerable than ever. At least at the hotel, a desk clerk saw to it that men did not get pass the elevator door. But here, how did I know he did not live in the building?

The stalking continued. He somehow got my new phone number and called often saying he was coming over to see me. Terrified, I'd hide in the bathroom, it being the only room that did not have a window. I hoped he would think that I was out and leave me alone. My new apartment became a prison I emerged from only to go to work. Weeks passed and nothing changed.

Every month, the landlord had a lady come in to clean the apartments. We were given the date ahead of time and asked not to be there during that time if possible. I had always tried to be gone when she came, but one day I arrived home before she finished.

"I'm sorry. I didn't mean to walk in while you are cleaning. Do you want me to leave?"

"No, honey, it's okay. I needed to talk to you anyway. I hate to just ask this way, but are you a Christian?"

"Yes, I am. Why do you ask?"

"Well, ever since you moved in here, the Lord has led

me to pray for the lady in apartment number six. He kept telling me that you are in danger."

I was touched, and a flicker of hope flared in my heart. I didn't know that God led people to pray for strangers. Did he really do that? If so, maybe things would get better. The lady continued in a kind voice, "The Lord didn't tell me why you were in danger, just that you are. Is there anything other than praying that I could do for you?"

I didn't tell her about the stalker. I did tell her that I would be getting married and moving out just as soon as my fiancé came home. She promised that she would continue to pray for my protection. It was a comfort to know that God was looking out for me. I felt better, but still, there are times you want to feel that a physical human is there for you.

As uninterested as I had been in getting married when Harold left, by the time he came home, I was desperate to be with someone. I had written him about the stalker, and his response had been typically Harold.

"When I get back, I'll fight him if I have to. He will leave you alone!" Now that he was back, it felt good to share my fear and feel protected.

Unaccountably, the day after Harold returned home, he told me he had seen a guy answering the stalker's description. The man had been in a fight with a sailor, and the police took him away in handcuffs. It was hard to believe it was over just like that, but I did not hear from or see the stalker again. Harold began to look like a man to lean on, and I figured I had made a good choice.

*D*ear *G*irls,

I cannot begin to tell you how important it is to truly know the man you are about to marry, because along with the wonderful things you may see in him, you will also be marrying his unmet needs, unhealed hurt, and unresolved issues. By now you can clearly see what a mass of psychological problems I struggled with, and your grandfather had his own demons to fight.

Harold was born when his parents were only sixteen and seventeen years old. Soon afterwards his father, Ted, was drafted to fight in World War II. His young mother, Shirley, was unable to cope with a colicky baby alone, so she dropped him off at Ted's mother's house. After saying, "Here, you take him," she walked out the door and was not seen again for four years.

Your great-great grandma Cramer did not go to church, but she was a good person and loved the abandoned baby. She often talked about sitting in the recliner all night with him on her shoulder when he had colic so he would sleep.

During the four years Shirley was gone, she got a divorce from Ted, married again, had another baby boy, and divorced his father. When Ted returned from war, they decided to get back together. Although his mother didn't want him, his father insisted that Harold live with them. She begrudgingly took him in, and he lived the rest of his life trying to get his mother to love him.

During the next few years, Shirley and Ted had four more kids: three boys and a girl. Ted became a truck driver, which kept him on the road a lot. As a child, your grandpa discovered he had a love and a talent for music. His mom was not impressed. To make him tough, she threatened to make him wear a dress and ribbons in his hair if he failed to pick fights with other boys. The musically gifted little boy became a bully to please his mom.

By the time Harold was a teenager, his parents were divorced again. Shirley, never the motherly type, went on with her life, and, as the oldest, Harold became a surrogate father for his brothers and sister. He was expected to do the grocery shopping, housework, and take care of the kids. As he got older, he had to take one or more of his brothers with him on his dates. Her control and abuse lasted until he went into the navy.

His time in service and being stationed in Long Beach, where he met David, was the first time he had been free to be himself. With freedom came the delightful sense of humor that had so intrigued us. In the presence of the happy Harold, you would never guess that underneath all that fun was an insecure boy with no self-esteem and a pitiful desire to be accepted by his mother.

Had I known what to look for, I would have been able to glimpse the wounded side of your grandpa in his letters. I received this one soon after he left for sea duty.

> My Dearest,
>
> I hope you receive my letter and card on your birthday and it makes your day a little happier. I sure wish I could be with you, hold you in my arms and give you a great big birthday kiss. Marilyn, a lot of times when I was back in the states going out with you I felt pretty bad because I didn't have a

car. I was almost always broke and we had to spend most of our time walking around or at a movie. I thought eventually you would give up on me.

But you didn't and all the time we dated you never complained but I was worried. Do you know why I was worried? Well it's because you are very beautiful and you're just as sweet and kind as can be. I noticed a lot of guys really admire you as we walked down the streets. They all probably had more than me and could really give you a real good time. I always thought someday you would meet one of these guys. Well I don't quite understand why, but it makes me feel so proud you're my girl. And it looks as though you will be for always.

Sweetheart, I wish I could give you everything in the whole world. And there are so many things I want to do for you. But yet you seem to be satisfied with just my love. I thank the Lord for this every night. I never knew I could be so happy. I really think I'm the luckiest guy in the world. And you know if you love me as I love you and you continue, and we keep close to God no matter what happens in the future, if the time comes when we are sad, worried or disappointment we'll always really have happiness.

Love,
Harold

Of course, when we marry someone, we only see what we want to see. I saw a man who said he loved me and would take care of me, but I didn't see the wounds from his past.

---

*D*ear *G*irls,

*W*hen your grandpa-to-be came home, he came bearing gifts. Among them was a three-foot-tall stuffed panda, a dozen red roses, a complete set of Noritake china, a set of silverware, a stereo system, record player, and an engagement ring. I accepted them all, and we planned a small wedding at the church I attended when I lived with James and Marilyn. Another navy couple would stand up for us.

I wanted to get married because I was afraid to be alone. I wanted a home. I wanted all the pain inside to go away. Harold seemed to be my best option. Like many girls, I thought marriage would be the answer to all my troubles. Like many girls, I was dead wrong.

The truth is marriage only magnifies your unresolved issues; it does not solve them. Your grandfather and I both had severely dysfunctional childhoods, and like every couple on the face of the earth we brought our past into our future. Our expectations about marriage and each other were solidly grounded in all the negatives of our past. What we didn't have as children, we expected married life to give to us. It was too much to ask of any one person or relationship.

My expectations were a little airy. For instance, as a small girl I had watched a show on television where a lady was wearing a beautiful evening gown and a tiara. All my growing up years, I daydreamed about dressing up as a pretty princess, but there had been no school dances, no proms, no pretty dresses, only hand-me-downs. The little child in me figured getting married was my only chance to wear a pretty princess gown.

As for the daily ins and outs of marriage, I had been in the home of my captors for so long I had no grand illusions of romance and prince charming. I figured the only difference for me would be that the two of us would live our lives under the same roof. Two people doing their own thing. Oh, I knew that I would still be called upon to fix the meals, clean the house etc. Only difference is this time I would call the shots, so to speak, and not be pressured into making sure things were perfect. Never again would I be yelled at or threatened.

Furthermore, my workload would be entirely up to me. No unauthorized babysitting to do out of obligation. Oh sure, I would have children, and I would want them to have those things I never had. Not so much material things, but the intangibles that were denied me. They would come home from school and see a mommy cooking in the kitchen. They would be allowed to go places and have friends.

My idealistic notions began to unravel even before the wedding. With dreamy-eyed excitement I visited the bridal departments of different stores until I found my dress. It was perfect in every way, the fit, the style, the fabric. I was a princess. Carefully, I placed the white vision of loveliness back on its padded hanger and carried it to the cashier with money in hand. She took one look at me and said, "You cannot buy this dress without your parents here." I stared at her in disbelief. *What kind of conspiracy was this? Parents? I had no parents.*

I protested, but the department manager confirmed that it was the store policy to forbid anyone underage to purchase a wedding dress without parental consent. I did look younger than my eighteen years, but I could not prove my age. I refused to ask James to sign for me. When Harold had invited him and Esther to the wedding, they said they were busy that day. With no recourse, I settled on a simple green suit and decided to deal as I always had. What was one more disappointment? It was a way of life.

Harold and I made an appointment for a premarital counseling session with my old pastor, the one who helped when Marilyn committed suicide. When we showed up, the church secretary told us pastor wasn't there. Then she cheerily said, "His wife asked him to go shopping with her so he looked up your attendance record at church and found out that over the years you were here almost all the time! So he said to tell you that anyone who attends church every Sunday could not possibly have any problems!" Yeah right.

Unfortunately, this is an all-too common assumption, yet all I had were problems, and church attendance hadn't fixed me. Most of my contact with the religious world was much like this incident. In my journey toward healing, I kept looking for someone in the church to see past my façade and recognize that deep inside I was dying.

The day of the wedding seemed like just another day. I put on the plain green suit and waited for Harold to pick me up for the ceremony. On the way to the church, we got a flat tire and were a half hour late. When we finally arrived, the pastor was waiting along with the navy couple and James and Esther, who had changed their minds about coming. After the ceremony, we opened our one gift and cut a two-layer wedding cake made from a boxed mix. A few pictures were snapped, and that was it.

We could not afford a honeymoon and continued to live at my place until we found a one-bedroom walkup close to the base. While moving in, we left the box containing our wedding pictures and negatives on the sidewalk. In the three minutes it took to go upstairs and come back down, someone stole them all. It was just as well; the whole wedding thing was as off kilter as the marriage. It was as if we were sent off to war with no training and no weapons. We never stood a chance.

---

*D*ear *G*irls,

I survived years of abuse by building walls around my emotions, but as the years rolled on those walls did nothing to protect me from more wounds. Even though I had no romantic notions about marriage, I wasn't beyond being hurt and disappointed at the way our life together evolved.

Please don't misunderstand; I do not mean to blame your grandpa for my ongoing problems or downgrade his good points. We both were deeply wounded people, and wounded people wound others. Most of the time, we were so blinded by our own pain we could not see the other's empty heart. Our unresolved issues hooked up like homing pigeons and began to manifest early on.

You may recall my expectation of marriage went something like this: We would be two people living together but doing our own thing. I would call the shots as to what I would do and when. I would not be pressured, and I would never again be yelled at or threatened. You may also remember I went into this relationship with the twisted view that I could somehow atone for Marilyn's death by saving him from the same fate.

So my underlying aim was to succeed where I had failed before. I didn't want to be controlled ever again, but I was willing to do anything to keep him happy. Yes, I know that makes no sense, but I had no idea how to make sense of my world.

Because he had never been loved and validated, your grandpa's whole purpose in life was geared toward guaranteeing he would be the controlling factor. In order to never be hurt again, he had to be the boss. All knowledge began and ended with him. He alone decided what we would do and when we would do it. My opinion did not matter. He had all the answers, and if I disagreed with him, well I was just wrong. The whole situation was a recipe for the ongoing disaster that continued for twenty-five years.

A few months before he got out of service, I gave birth to Libby's mother. On a Sunday morning three weeks before she was due, I woke up in labor. I told Harold to call the doctor and get ready to take me to the hospital. His response was, "I guess this means that you won't be fixing my breakfast?"

He then informed me that it was false labor and he was going out for donuts. His mother always had false labor, so it had to be the same for me. On his way out, he sent our neighbor up from downstairs. She had experience having babies and confirmed that I was really in labor and called the doctor. When Harold returned, she insisted he take me to the hospital, and much to his annoyance she refused to let him take the time to eat his donuts. Forty-five minutes later, our beautiful baby girl was born.

She was the most beautiful baby I had ever seen, perfect in every way. I named her Abigail and quickly began to build my world around her. The only problem was that I did not have the foggiest notion of how to be a mother. All the information I had for what I considered real mothering came from old television series like *Father Knows Best* and *Leave It to Beaver*. Other than that, I had to ask her dad even simple things, like how warm to have the bottle. What I did know was she was going to have everything I never had as a child. My little girl would have a mommy to cook dinner, take her to the park, and buy her pretty Easter dresses. Of course, I would let her have lots of friends.

After your grandpa was discharged, he wanted to live near his family in Tennessee. We packed our baby and all our worldly possessions into our 1957 turquoise and white Chevy. The three-foot-tall panda your Grandpa brought back from Japan sat in the front seat. You should have seen the double takes people gave us as we passed them on the road. We looked like two kids taking their stuffed Panda for a ride.

The trip was long, and the car was old with a tendency to overheat. We stopped to fill the radiator as often as we did to fill the gas tank. I was young and naïve enough to be looking forward to settling down with my husband and little baby into a normal life surrounded by a loving family. It was there that the rest of my idealistic expectations about marriage unraveled.

---

*D*ear *G*irls,

*M*eeting my new husband's family for the first time was both nerve-wracking and interesting. The most interesting element by far was Grandma Cramer. If you remember, she was the one who took care of your grandpa the first four years of his life. I could tell right away that Grandma was quite a character and definitely one of a kind.

Bright eyed, slim, and quite youthful, her real age was a well-kept secret. Grandma dyed her gray hair jet black and dressed like a bag lady totally unconcerned with what she wore or, for that matter, what you might think about what she wore. Her signature outfit was plaid polyester pants with elastic waistbands, topped with a blouse that never matched her bottoms and most of the time defied description. Grandma was mixing plaids and prints in wild colors before the hippies of the sixties even thought about it. I guess you could say she was a trendsetter.

The look worked for her and shaved years off her age. She once applied for a job at a factory and was hired, but before her first day she made the mistake of asking how this job would effect her Social Security payments. They told her they did not realize she was that old and reneged on the job offer.

When she started dating after her husband died, she informed her family, "Although I love you all dearly, if you see me out on a date, I will not acknowledge you as any relation to me." One night, one of her sons saw her out with a gentleman friend and walked over to the table. She quickly introduced him as a neighbor who just happened to have the same last name as her.

All her grandchildren adored her, knowing they were always welcome to stop by anytime and help themselves to the hamburger patties she kept in her freezer for them. Those same kids loved playing tricks on her and once put a copy of the book *Sin, Sex and Self-Control* in her front room window for all the world to see.

Going out in public with Grandma was a trip and a half, as well as a calculated risk. One day I went shopping with her because none of the other family members were available. The real truth is they had been there done that too many times to voluntarily put themselves in such a situation again. So I was elected and soon discovered that shopping with Grandma took three times as long as it needed to because of her tendency to comment loudly and long about the price of everything. By the time we got to Burger King for lunch, I was exhausted, and she was as spry as ever.

Over burgers and fries, she informed me that the only thing she loved about old age was that you could be as ornery as you wanted and no one seemed to mind.

"To prove my point," she added as she dipped a fry in ketchup, "I am going to walk out of this restaurant with one of those plastic trays just to prove I can get by with it." To my dismay she did it! As she tucked the stolen tray into the car, she warned me, "Girly, you couldn't get away with something like that, so don't try."

Gifts from Grandma were always a hoot. We couldn't decide if she was just being funny or stingy. Every year, the whole family gathered at her house for the holidays, and she always had a gift neatly wrapped up for each of her grandchildren. Libby, the Christmas your mother was fourteen, she opened her present from Grandma to find a box of Efferdent (a cleaner for false teeth) and a bottle of Geritol (a tonic older people used which was advertised as having "twice the iron as in a pound of calf's liver"). I knew Grandma was on a roll when I untied my pretty red box and found a dress somebody's great-grandma may have worn twenty years earlier, and, Rylee, your mom, who was five at the time, got a tube of toothpaste and a coin purse which had seen better days. The rest of the family received similar gifts. We all got a good laugh out of it.

I am sure you will not be surprised to find out that one of Grandma's favorite pastimes was going to secondhand stores. Once, after we moved back to California, Harold's father brought her to see us. I told Grandma Cramer since this was her first visit to the area I would take her wherever she wanted to go and suggested Disneyland, Knott's Berry Farm, the Pacific Ocean, or maybe the San Diego Zoo. Nope, she wasn't interested in any of those.

"I know!" she chirped. "You can take me to the nearest Goodwill Store." So I loaded her into our brand-new car and off we went to the Goodwill so she could buy another pair of plaid polyester pants, which she could not possibly have lived without. She was thrilled with her California fashion find, although they looked suspiciously like the Tennessee version she had on.

We did get her to Disneyland, but the only thing she liked there was the Carousel of Progress showing how things had changed over the years. With each new scene, she pointed out the stuff she still had in her home.

Her other favorite pastime was reading *True Confession*,

you know those magazines with stories like: "I Knocked My Husband in the Head Because He Looked at Me Cross-eyed" or "Exactly What Happened on My Wedding Night?" and "Old Enough to Be His Mother." Unlike some grandmas of that era, she never hid her steamy magazines under the couch cushions but piled them on the end tables in plain sight.

Grandma Cramer was indeed a piece of work, howbeit a delightful one. I can't say the same for my mother-in-law. Shirley picked up right where she left off before Harold went into the navy. She dumped her family on us. The only difference was Harold was not the only one stuck with the daily care of her kids.

At nineteen years old, I would never have guessed in a million years that I was entering a marriage where I would be called upon to be a stepmother for four children ages five to fourteen. Needless to say, the rest of my premarital expectation of "my work load being entirely up to me and no unauthorized babysitting out of obligation" bit the dust.

---

*D*ear *G*irls,

*A*fter our move, my position in the family soon became painfully clear. As a new bride, I looked forward to going shopping with my husband to choose items for our new home. It never happened. Harold asked his fourteen-year-old brother to go with him to pick out our furniture. I was left behind with the knowledge that my input wasn't needed or wanted.

Although his father paid child support, Harold was expected to supply any extra money the kids needed. He did it gladly, even if we had to do without. On the first Easter after our move, I was excited about buying my baby girl an Easter dress and getting one for myself. Somehow I blindly clung to the illusion that now that I was married I could make up for my deprived childhood. When I asked my husband for the money, his reaction flashed me right back to the time Marilyn bought the other little girls an Easter dress and told me I was not worthy to have one.

"Oh!" he exclaimed. "I almost forgot about Easter! I need to buy a new outfit for my sister and at least new shirts for the boys." As an afterthought, he added, "If there is any money left over, you can get a dress for you two." There was no money left over, and we did not get Easter dresses. Not only could I not make up for my deprived childhood, I was reliving it.

We had been there a few months when he promised his brothers to come over to their house on a Saturday afternoon to watch a football game. Saturday morning, I woke up in excruciating pain. Barely able to speak, I told

Harold something was wrong and I needed a doctor. He said, "You're faking it. Just get the baby dressed, her bag packed, and quit wasting my time." Somehow, I got everything together then was ordered, "Okay, get in the car," as he walked out the door. Doubled over in agony, I carried my six-month-old baby and her diaper bag to the car.

It was a good thing he planned to stop by Grandma's house to do an odd job for her before the game. She took one look at me and declared. "Harold, she needs a doctor."

"Don't have time right now; the boys are expecting me as soon as I finish up here," he said, going on with his work. In response, Grandma did not say a word. She turned on her heel, went into the kitchen, and returned holding her broom in the air like a ball bat. Then with unmistakable yet controlled anger she gave her grandson an ultimatum: "You will take her to the hospital right now. If you don't, I will beat you with this broom until you get out of my house, then I will see to it that she gets help."

Grandma was a persuasive woman when she got riled. In self-defense, Harold reluctantly agreed to take me to the hospital. Within an hour I was being prepped for an emergency appendectomy. When I came out from under the anesthesia, he was standing there over my bed demanding, "Well, how does it feel to be knifed?" From there he went into a tirade about how totally selfish I had been to think my need for surgery could ever outweigh the fact that he had missed watching the ballgame with his brothers. I stared at him through a haze of pain and something like grief.

No, your grandpa's reaction was not logical. Wounded

people have a hard time being logical. Like me, he had stayed emotionally the young age when his wounds were inflicted. As a little boy, his mom had stopped his plans for fun so many times that even as a theoretically grown-up husband and father he acted out of the psychological place of an eight-year-old boy. And he never saw it. A person can hide from himself the fact that he is terribly wounded, but he cannot hide the intensity of the feelings from his wounds.

Because of his inability to stand up to his mother, he became a tyrant in his own family. Years later, he could say something as ridiculous as, "I wish I could get my way just once!" That was the wounded little boy speaking; it had zero to do with his life with us. Actually, he never did have a life with us. He just lived his abused childhood over and over until he died, which was sad for him and sad for us, because all this wonderful insight into the whys of his actions and how they affected my own life and the lives of our children came long after he was gone. By then, all of us were wrapped in a cloak of shared darkness.

*D*ear *G*irls,

*L*iving with your grandpa was life on a dead run. I literally never knew where we would be from day to day. Like most hurting people, he looked for external things to take away the pain. Harold's addiction was change. It may sound strange to think of change as an addiction, but he had the same symptoms as any addict, the overwhelming urge, the utter disregard of the consequences, as well as an inability to stop.

Not understanding that the change he needed was internal, he was on a constant quest to find a place and a situation that would give him peace. Behind his rough, take-charge façade, his own self-talk went something like this: "No one loves me. My needs are never going to be met if I have to trust others. My next fix is the most important thing in my life." Harold's next fix was moving. Consequently, we had to be ready at a moment's notice to pack up and go. He had no real feelings for the damage he was inflicting upon his family. He simply figured if it was good for him it was good for everybody. We moved twenty-four times in the twenty-five years we were married.

Many of our moves vacillated between living in California and living near his family in Tennessee. If we lived in California, every day I heard how he had blown it and we should be near his family. Back in Tennessee, it was the same story. He would go on and on about how he had messed up again and we needed to live on the West Coast. One of these moves to Tennessee lasted a mere week before we were back in California. He could not find a happy medium. He felt he was either betraying his family by not being a resident father figure, or trapped by all the responsibilities.

Eventually, even living far away did not solve his problems or relieve him of the burden. Over the next eight years, no matter where we lived, the children were with us on a regular basis. Harold either invited them, or, without warning, his mother sent whichever children she wanted to be rid of at the moment and told him, "Take them, and I'll let you know when I want them back." We never knew if it was going to be one child or three, or if they were going to stay for a month or two years.

I was relegated to the position of a housekeeper or babysitter with no rights. One day, I said, "Harold it's such a pretty day; let's go on a picnic." He told me that was a really stupid idea. Not five minutes later, one of his brothers suggested the very same thing, and I heard, "Wonderful idea! Marilyn, get a picnic together; we're going to the park." When I asked him to teach me to drive a car, he said, "No, the car isn't good enough." The next day, his twelve-year-old brother wanted to learn to drive and the response was, "Sure, no problem!" He spent the whole day with him. It was another ten years before I learned to drive.

Now, I realize that his mother had controlled him so long and so brutally that he was psychologically unable to listen to a woman about anything, but back then I took it all personally. Resentment piled on top of resentment. What self-esteem I had not lost before, I was surely losing then. I could take no action to change the situation. I began to feel like an intruder in my own home. I had been emotionally paralyzed for a long time; now I was becoming a nonentity.

---

*D*ear *G*irls,

Your grandfather never had a problem getting a job as an electrician in different factories. He usually made good money, but his need to move and the added stress of taking care of his brothers and sister sometimes strained our finances to the limit. He let me take care of the money partly because he preferred to blame someone else for his problems and partly because he knew if I handled them he could spend as much as he wanted and I would never call him on it. It wouldn't matter if it was an urge to move halfway across the country, sell a house at a loss, or drive seventy miles to get a Coke.

I never said a word even though it would be up to me to work the magic and find the money to live on. When we were out, he always wanted to eat at restaurants. Many times, even when I was hungry, I wouldn't order anything so I wouldn't have to make that money up. Off and on over the years, I held a job simply to cover his urges and to help support his brothers and sister.

I tried so very hard to make everything work for Harold, but confrontation was beyond me. We were both so emotionally broken there was no way we could help each other. In reality, I was a codependent in his addictions. By allowing him to continue to act in unacceptable ways without a challenge, I was actually interrupting God's law of sowing and reaping. Sowing and reaping is one way we learn. If we do something and it brings about a negative result that hurts or humiliates us, we are more likely to change our behavior. When we are allowed to get away with harmful actions, we see no reason to change. Harold had no reason to reconsider how he acted. He suffered no immediate repercussions for his choices. He was sowing and I was reaping.

My voice had been silenced as a child, and as an adult my husband made it clear that I had nothing to add to any conversation. On the rare occasions I dared to speak up and ask for something, such as wanting to learn to drive, I was ignored. When this happens to a person consistently, they lose a sense of their own identity.

At the same time, buried deep inside was the woman I was meant to be, the real me. The real me wanted to climb on top of a table and scream, "Does anyone know I exist? I am a human being, and even though my emotions do not show, that does not mean that I have no feelings." But the courage to do that would take years in coming, and in the meantime I lived my life as if in a silent tomb, shut away, forgotten. One of the dangers of being in this state of mind is the accompanying thought of *You're already dead; suicide is not such a big deal*.

Over the years, I have heard people ask women like me, "So why did you put up with it?" Not a bad question, until you realize that women like me do not know how to do anything else. People can only act out of what is deposited into their souls. I had no frame of reference to be any other way. I was much like the elephant chained when he was a baby. He tries and tries to escape but cannot. Eventually, his spirit is broken, and he gives up. By then even a small rope can hold him to a flimsy stake in the ground. No matter how strong he becomes, no matter how easily broken the rope around his leg, he is still in prison. Onlookers wonder, *Why is he letting them do this to him?* Yes, the elephant could physically walk away, but his childhood experience tells him he is trapped with no recourse. The way I lived was all I knew.

---

*D*ear *G*irls,

*D*uring all my years of emotional slavery, we went to church as a family and maintained a relationship with God. True, from my years with Marilyn and James, some of my concepts of him were still seriously twisted. Marilyn's theology of works and James's take on being a deacon in good standing while sexually molesting little girls had damaged me.

Another element that kept me in spiritual and emotional bondage was meditating on how others might perceive me. Somewhere along the way someone had said to me, "You are young and resilient, and you will bounce back." Through the years, that thought swirled over and over through my soul until I was ultimately convinced that I was less than other people because my ability to bounce back was just beyond me.

I was sure others felt it was some failure on my part that I couldn't get over the past. I tried to get free. I read books, prayed, and listened to ministers who kept saying, "Just get over it" and "Pull yourself up by your boot straps." Well, I didn't know how to get over it, and my boot straps were so frayed I couldn't find them anymore.

Eventually I learned that bouncing back has everything to do with how inflated your ball is. If you don't get enough air deposited in your ball, bouncing back is not even an option. God ultimately was able to fill my ball with enough air of his love and promises that I became the healed woman I am today.

But it was a long journey, and my faith in spiritual

leaders—which was damaged as a child—dissipated along the way. In fact, my lack of confidence in pastors was so pronounced that I was literally afraid to get baptized. I thought he might drown me. Honestly. I had heard a joke about a man who suddenly found himself at the pearly gates requesting St. Peter to allow him into heaven. St. Peter asked the guy if he was saved. The punch line of the joke confirmed my fears: "Yes," he assured him, "as a matter of fact, I was getting baptized. Now, at our church, we do not believe in any of that sprinkling stuff, so we go all the way under. The last thing I remember was the preacher dunked me and held me down so long I never came up, and here I am."

Laugh if you must, girls, but it had been my experience that ministers could not be trusted to look out for my best interest. I was convinced that given the chance a preacher would do me in. And yet I so wanted to do what the Bible said about being baptized.

We had been married about five years when your grandpa said he was going to be baptized at our church's upcoming baptismal service. This was my chance. We could be baptized together arm in arm and go down at the same time. A lay person would have to help Pastor, so I made sure that I was on the lay person's side. I figured if Pastor did try to drown me at least your Grandpa would be there to stop him. All went well, and I survived being baptized in water.

Codependency, trust issues, and twisted theology were ongoing problems, but in other areas, my faith could be strong, and I was able to pray and hear from God. In spite of our ongoing issues, our young family experienced some things that could only be categorized as miracles.

During her first four years of life, Abigail came down with severe tonsillitis about every six weeks. I pleaded with the doctor to remove them, but he refused. One night at church someone preached about divine healing. It struck me that God could heal my child. I had her prayed for, and she never had tonsillitis again.

Another miracle was Hannah, Rylee's mother. Abigail was nine years old when her sister was born. She too was sweet and beautiful in every way. I adored her. It was not until she was eight months old that I began to suspect that something was wrong. While lying on her back, she would hold her little hands out as if to brace herself for a fall and then cry as if she was scared.

After a series of tests, the doctor informed us that she had epilepsy and was having seizures eighty percent of the time. Furthermore, we needed to be prepared for the fact that she would never get well and she would never be able to live any kind of a normal life. The following Sunday morning, we had the church pray for her. While they were praying, I felt the Lord speak to my heart that she would be healed in time. And I simply believed it.

I continued taking Hannah for regular medical check-ups. The doctor and I did not see eye to eye on his prognosis. He kept reminding me that I was looking through rose-colored glasses if I ever thought that she would get well. I protested that she was going to get better and be healed. While I could not stand up to Harold, something deep inside me would not allow that doctor to say those things about my baby girl.

Hannah was sick for about a year and a half before I felt the Lord again speak to me about her healing. I had just come home from a Sunday night service when, beyond all reasoning, I knew she would be healed the next day. I felt led to call a guy who once worked with Harold and have him pray for her. Roy had gone into the ministry about the time we moved out of that state, and I had no idea how to find him. I finally got in touch with an old acquaintance in that state and asked if she could track him down for me. An hour later, she called back with a phone number.

The voice on the other end of the line said, "Hello, Juvenile Center."

I hesitated for a minute, then asked, "May I please speak to Roy?"

"Oh, you want the chaplain; just a minute please."

"Roy, this is Harold's wife. I don't know if you remember me or not, but since I last saw you we had another daughter. She has epilepsy, and the doctor gives her no hope of getting better. I believe the Lord wants you to pray for her and she will be healed. Since we live a thousand miles away, you have to do this over the phone."

Without hesitation, Roy began to pray. After saying amen, his parting line was, "You know the Lord had been dealing with me for a few months now that I should go into a healing ministry. I guess you just confirmed that. Nobody ever calls juvenile center when they have a sick baby."

As far as I was concerned, Hannah was healed. The next day, I had an appointment to talk to a social worker. In our state, if you had a child with two different things wrong with her, you were automatically assigned a social worker, who had the job of pointing you in the right direction.

"Now, as I understand it, your daughter has epilepsy and delayed learning. Is that correct?"

"No," I responded boldly. "She did have epilepsy, but the Lord healed her yesterday, and now I guess that she only has delayed learning."

"Do you want to tell me about her healing? Did you take her to a faith healer or what?"

I recounted how it all came about and ended with, "Roy prayed for her over the phone, and now she is healed."

To my surprise, he smiled and said, "That's great! I am a Christian too and believe in divine healing. The state, however, does not recognize miracles, so as far as they are concerned, your daughter has two problems. This makes her eligible for enrollment in the school for handicap children. They have a physical therapist and a speech therapist. We can sign her up when school starts in September."

The following night, I went to church and shared about Hannah's healing. When service was over, a lady came up to me.

"I have to ask. Who is Hannah's doctor?" After giving her the answer, she laughed out loud. "I love it! This is an answer to prayer for my girlfriend. My girlfriend has been dating your doctor for about six months now. She has been trying to tell him about the Lord and wanting him to go to church with her. His holdout is that they believed in divine healing. He made a comment that until he sees one of his patients healed, he will not accept the Lord."

She then asked when we would see the doctor again. "Hannah has an appointment with him next week."

When I showed up for the appointment, the first thing he said was, "I heard that the Lord healed her."

"That's right. He did," I affirmed without hesitation.

"Are you willing to prove it? It is about time for you to take her in for another EEG. If I schedule you one, will you take her in?"

"Of course I will."

When the test results came back, the doctor called me personally.

"Marilyn," he began, "I don't know what to tell you, other than I guess your God does heal."

Hannah never had another seizure and was able to catch up quickly from the effects of the learning disability.

*D*ear *G*irls,

*M*y last letter may be confusing if you do not understand how a person full of psychological baggage and misinformation can at times hear the voice of God. The reality is a person's soul can operate on different levels, depending on what was programmed into it. In my friend Wanda Winters-Gutierrez's book, *The Search for Peace*, she explains how this can happen. "Every person is a spirit being, they have a soul (which is made up of their mind, will, and emotions) and they live in a body. Our soul is like a computer, it only knows whatever is programmed into it. Whatever is deposited into it, will eventually be downloaded into our lives. Pain in, pain out; love in, love out; acceptance in, acceptance out; rejection in, rejection out. This programming constitutes our core beliefs. A core belief is not necessarily the truth, but wounded people live as if they were irrefutable and unchangeable."

She goes on to say, "When we have experienced rejection, abuse, or trauma the 'core belief' deposited in our souls (or mind, will and emotions) can be wrong, warped and fundamentally self-destructive." A person can have a part of his inner belief system full of negative core beliefs and another part can be full of faith and power. She calls it having a fragmented soul.

Somewhere along the line, I had picked up enough positives about God that I could at times hear his voice and have real faith. At other times, in my downward spiral of misery, my programming had produced such negative beliefs that I fought for my sanity. And no one ever knew.

The truth is abused and abusing people can appear fine on the outside—adjusted, even happy and peaceful, but if you could see their souls, you would find a dark chasm full of pain. If they continue to stuff anger and hurt into that cold darkness, the results can be catastrophic. When their soul reaches its capacity of damage, they snap. At that point, you will find even Christians giving in to thoughts of murder or suicide. For me, murder wasn't an option. Suicide was another matter.

---

*D*ear *G*irls,

*B*efore we found out about Hannah's illness, we had moved from California to Washington State. It was the beginning of winter, and the sun in that part of the country was a phenomenon we only saw about sixty days a year. With no sun and the overcast skies endlessly dripping moisture, I stayed chilled to the bone. The first three weeks, we lived with a family Harold knew until we found an apartment where we lived for about two months while we waited for our house in California to sell. When we closed on the California place, Harold bought a large two-story house in need of a major yard renovation.

Although I had become quite adept at moving, this one was nearly beyond me. It was about then I realized that something was wrong with Hannah and had her diagnosed. She became very attached to me, not wanting me out of her sight. If I went into the bathroom, she sat outside the door and cried until I came out. She only slept about three hours before she woke up wanting to be held. Her awake time lasted for two or three more hours, and then we would start the process all over again. Most nights, I got less than four hours of sleep. Harold refused to help. Taking care of children was woman's work, and I was pretty stupid if I couldn't take care of one little baby by myself.

Evidently yard work was also woman's work. Besides taking care of a ten-year-old, a sick baby, a demanding husband, cooking, cleaning, grocery shopping, laundry, moving, and setting up the house, I was also expected to help him work on our new lawn. On his day off, while Abigail watched Hannah, we raked leaves, cut brush, chopped out tree roots, and prepared the soil for grass seed. We worked nonstop until it was time for me to get lunch, and then we began again until it was time for me to fix dinner.

This went on week after endless week. Eventually, sheer muscle-aching, foggy-brained exhaustion overcame me. All I wanted to do was sleep. Since that did not appear to be an option, I became preoccupied with thoughts of suicide. It is said that suicide is not chosen; it simply happens when pain exceeds a person's resources for coping. I believe it. I had nothing left. I had been dead for a long time, and my body needed to rest.

A friend asked me if I ever journaled.

"No," I told her. "Unless you count suicide notes as journaling." I wrote piles of them. After I was gone, I wanted everyone left behind to know why I chose this path. I wanted someone to care, to feel guilty, to be sorry. After carefully detailing my pain and everybody else's shortcomings, I tore the notes up. It really didn't matter anyway. Nobody cared.

I was coming home from the grocery store the first time the urge to end it all became overwhelming. As I approached an overpass, I could see myself making a hard right and plunging the car over the edge. There was no reason not to. It would end the loneliness and pain; I could rest. The windshield wipers swished back and forth as the car rolled toward the edge of the bridge. I had no power to stop myself. This was it. It was over.

Suddenly something happened. I was in my own lane, hands steady on the wheel, moving safely to the other side of the overpass and going home. That night, I got a call from David. He had been out of the service since Abigail was born. He lived in California and was involved in counseling ministry, so in a previous call I had shared with him about the depression. He had promised to pray for me.

When I answered the phone the evening of the overpass incident, he cut straight to the chase. "Hey Sis. What's up with you? God showed me you driving off an overpass this afternoon. I prayed for you." The time of his prayer corresponded exactly with the moment I had found myself with steady hands on the wheel pulling back into my lane.

A year later, we sold the two-story house, packed up, and moved one city over into a one-story house. Of course, it was a fixer-upper, and we had to finish off the basement and add a bath and a bedroom. And did I mention we had to plant grass and fix up the yard there as well? We were there nine months when Harold decided to move back to Tennessee to be near his family. I dreaded the very thought of living there again, but he applied for a job and waited for the final okay.

We rented an apartment in case we needed it after the house closed and before the job came through. I was in the midst of packing when he got the bright idea to drive to Tennessee for the weekend. It took us two days and nights to get there, and he planned to stay one day before driving back to Washington state.

Although we had only one week to move, the day we cleared escrow on the house Harold told me we were going on a two-day camping trip with the church group. They were planning to have a worship service and a time of fellowship, and it would be fun, or so I was told. I didn't want to go. It was cold. I was tired. I still had packing to do. I didn't know how I would find the energy to do the whole tent-campfire-cooking-taking-care-of-the-girls thing by myself while he socialized. But we went.

I decided to kill myself that weekend. Along with our camping gear, I packed a bottle of tranquilizers Harold took for his nerves. I figured that I would just overdose. No mess. Just go to sleep and never wake up. Simple. Right? Actually not so simple.

The whole weekend I was never alone. If it wasn't Harold demanding something, it was the girls or the other campers always around talking, talking, talking. I couldn't find a moment to even swallow the pills. During the worship service, I slipped away and headed for the restroom. This time, I was determined. I had the tranquilizers in my hand and was ready to take them when a child from the church walked into the restroom. You can't kill yourself in front of a little kid. It was no use. With a sigh I gave up and dropped the pills back in my purse. Then I went back to the worship service and all the happy smiling people who thought they knew me.

*D*ear *G*irls,

A few days after the campout, your grandpa came down with pneumonia. I thought it served him right for insisting that we go on the campout, but my attitude changed two days later when I received the same diagnosis. Just to show you, once again how a fragmented soul can work on two levels, check this out. Both of us being down at the same time did not work for your grandpa, so he told me that I couldn't be sick because he needed me to take care of him. Furthermore, he was going to pray that I would be healed. Sure enough, I got well enough to nurse him back to health.

We had to move the next weekend. Harold was still sick, so the folks at church stepped in and moved us into the apartment. Three weeks later, the job came through, and we were on our way to a city in Tennessee, seventy-five miles from his family. We rented a duplex for a year and then were able to build a house and actually lived in it six whole years. It was during those six years that my healing process began.

In later years when I was trying to sort the suicide thing out in my mind, I found a list of possible reasons people take their own life. Research shows that any one of them can bring on suicidal thoughts; I had twelve. Besides the utter exhaustion and inability to cope with my daily life, the list included a feeling of powerlessness, ongoing abuse, a life permanently changed by an event, social isolation, a sense of unfairness that people were not there to help me, inability to experience the joys of life, lost sense of self, unexpressed rage at those who should have helped me, memory lapses for parts of a traumatic event, and the inner stress of denial.

Denial was a big one for me. It had come in handy as a child when I had found myself in the midst of terrible situations. Denial made the pain go away. It was a survival tool. Unfortunately, it is also one of the most difficult psychological conditions to deal with. The more old pain and feelings we have stuffed, the more difficult it is to break through. I had a thirty-year history of internalizing my feelings and denying their reality. Denial by itself can kill you, and I had lived in enough denial to do me in a couple a dozen times.

The suicidal depression came and went for a while until one Sunday morning the pastor at our new church said, "God wants to deliver some people. If anyone has anything they want to be delivered of, just stand to your feet where you are and tell God what you need." I stood to my feet and told God I needed to be healed from depression. Never again was I tempted to commit suicide.

*D*ear *G*irls,

*A*fter we moved into our house, things were much easier for a number of reasons. Besides the deliverance from depression, there was no more packing and moving. The girls were healthy and doing well in school. Harold's brothers and sister were now grown and no longer stayed with us. Without all the work and stress, I was beginning to regain my health and move slowly toward wholeness.

Up until this time, I had held a deep conviction that I was broken apart inside and there were too many missing pieces to ever be put back together again. When you spend a long time without speaking openly, you fall into an aura of invisibility. For me, my struggle had reverted back to survival state. As the years passed, I had grown more silent and cynical, but now something was changing. Out of some miniscule fragment of my soul, healing had begun to manifest in such subtle ways I didn't recognize it at first.

While I was moving into a place of healing, your grandpa's nerves got worse. He began to suffer panic attacks and multiple illnesses, real and imaginary. He resented my health.

"If I were you, Marilyn," he would say, "I would get down on my knees every night and thank God that you don't have the problems I do! And I will tell you something else. These panic attacks are hereditary, so get used to them. Both of the girls will have them also." I let him rant on but dismissed that thought from my mind. Right then and there I chose not to accept that negative possibility into the lives of my girls. I knew God would take care of my children.

The coming wholeness manifested itself every once in a while when I stood up to your grandfather for treating me badly. I will never forget the first time I confronted him.

He was watching television and said, "Hey, Marilyn, this television has lines running up and down the picture. Get your coat and go buy a new one."

"Why don't we just take it in to the repair shop?" I said. "It seems like it would be simple to fix; other than the lines, it is still good."

"So you want to get it fixed? All right, fix it!" he yelled and began kicking the television screen with his steel-toed boot, trying to break it. When his foot slipped, the nineteen-inch set sank into the drywall.

Of course, this only served to infuriate him more, so he picked up the TV with both hands, reared back, and aimed it at the glass patio door. He had forgotten that it was still plugged in to both the wall and the VCR. It landed on the floor beside him.

"Marilyn, you are so stupid!" he screamed. "I can't believe it! You think that getting it fixed is better than getting a new one! You owe me an apology for not letting me buy one like I wanted to! I'm waiting! Are you going to apologize or not?"

Out of I-know-not-where, I said, "Harold, you are the one who owes me an apology for calling me stupid."

"Marilyn, you either apologize to me right now, or I am leaving and going to get a hotel room! I'm going to stay there until you decide to apologize to me!"

When I didn't answer, he demanded, "Did you hear what I said about me leaving?" I nodded my head that I had. He was taken aback and finally figured out I was not about to apologize, and he backed down.

"Okay, I will apologize to you this once. I'm sorry, but mark my words; I will never again apologize to you for anything else as long as I live. Do you get that?" He then picked up the television and took it to the repair shop. The lines in the television were fixed with a minor adjustment and a few dollars. The damage to the wall cost him eighty bucks. It was not easy to move out of a lifetime of victimization and silence into becoming the woman I was meant to be, but the journey had begun.

---

*D*ear *G*irls,

*M*y becoming whole was not in your grandpa's comfort zone. The few times I was able to stand up to him undermined his need to be in control. Psychologists say a wounded person will be drawn to recreate the emotional atmosphere they were brought up in. In Harold's case, he identified so much with his controlling mother that he became his mother. In my case, I had always been controlled, so that was the only kind of situation my wounded soul knew. We know that water will seek its own level; so do wounded souls. Our souls flowed out like water and found their own level in each other. In a situation like this, all goes well, in a sick dysfunctional way until one of the parties begins getting well.

As I began to step out of the shadows of my past, Harold unconsciously sensed he was no longer in control. His own insecurities surfaced, and when a pretty younger woman at work started paying attention to him he was flattered. He said they were just friends and he felt sorry for her because her husband was abusive. Imagine that. In reality he had found another victim.

I met her at the company picnic when he asked if she and her kids could go around with us for the rides. He said since she was a single parent it was the Christian thing to do to help her with her kids. Right. As far as my feelings were concerned, by now I knew that there was no hope for our marriage. I was actually past caring.

Their relationship lasted about a year. Then your grandpa did one of his famous one eighties and asked me if I wanted to renew our marriage vows. I was shocked. "I got to thinking about when we got married," he said one day out of the blue. "We didn't really have a large wedding. What do you say if we renew our vows this spring on our twentieth anniversary?"

He wanted it to be a proper wedding. I could get the wedding dress of my dreams, invitations, a wedding cake, a reception, anything I wanted. Quickly slipping into my denial mode, I hurried up and agreed before he had time to change his mind. How exciting! I felt like a new bride again, making all of the arrangements. I also felt this was a practice run as Abigail, who was eighteen, planned on getting married the next year.

She went shopping with me, and we found the perfect dress with a long train, sheer white sleeves, and lots of lacy ruffles. She said she wanted to wear it for her own wedding. How ideal! A real mother-daughter thing. It felt almost normal.

The girls were part of the wedding party and looked beautiful in their pretty new dresses. Harold wore a tuxedo, and, unknown to me, had made arrangements for us to go on a short three-day honeymoon. It was everything I ever dreamed.

Not long ago, I was telling a friend about this, and since she knew my and Harold's history together she asked, "So what do you think motivated him to step so far out of character and come up with this romantic notion?" I had one answer. "Guilt."

Actually, the renewing of our vows was just one more of those new beginnings that keep abused women holding on. They buy us off with a smile, a flower, a kiss on the neck, or a wedding. A flurry of hope flutters in our soul; maybe this time things would be different. Maybe.

Not long after that, your grandpa and I were watching a movie about an IRS agent no one liked. He sexually abused his wife and daughter, at the end of the movie his son killed him. This too-close-to-home plot brought a flood of emotions I couldn't hide. When Harold asked me what was wrong, I told him about James sexually abusing me all those years. Big mistake. In typical male fashion, when faced with someone else's problem, he immediately took it upon himself to fix it.

"I read in a book that you need to confront the abuser right away. Let me call David and he can confront James."

"No, no! Please, Harold. I'm not ready for this. I need time…don't…please don't. I can't! I just can't!" I begged. I pleaded. I cried. But there was no stopping him. He called David, and while he was at it, he told our teenage daughter Abigail because "she had a right to know." I was devastated.

The whole week he wouldn't leave it alone. He moved from simply trying to fix it to asking me a million questions and giving me advice on what I should have done. "Exactly what did he do? Why haven't you said something before? Why did you let him? If it were me, I would have…How come you didn't…You should have…You could have…" and on and on until I felt like I was on trial and needed to defend myself. By the end of the week, I thought I would go stark raving mad if he didn't shut up.

Sunday morning at church, the pastor said, "There are people here who are going through a really rough time right now and feel they might lose their mind." He asked them to stand, and one by one, he prayed for us. When he came to me, he asked God to give me ten times the strength I now possessed. Only God knew that it would take more strength than I had ever had to get through the next few years.

Dear Girls,

The return of my memory began as intrusions. Out of nowhere, a thought would surface. *I wonder what color eyes my real mom had? Was she blond like me? Was she quiet and shy or outgoing and full of fun? Tall or short?* Then there were the bigger questions. *Did I have brothers and sisters? Why hadn't my real parents come after me when Marilyn and James took me away? Didn't they care?*

Answers do not always come on a silver tray or in a rosy cloud. This is especially true if you are dealing with a deeply wounded soul. To get to my healing, I had to get out of the denial and be able to accept the truth about my past. That was no easy pill to swallow. The road to truth led through a dark, dark place in my psyche and was littered with nightmares, secrets, and half truths.

The nightmares were horrifying. *It is 3 a.m. I'm sitting up in bed, staring wide eyed into the darkness trembling. It had seemed so real. I was standing outside a house looking into a window. I can see a man and a woman. She is facing me. I can see the man's back and the knife in his hand plunging downward.* Then blankness set in, and I woke up.

In another dream, I as in the same place looking at the lady. *I see a fountain of blood pulsating down her chest. I am mesmerized until I noticed the blood is flowing so profusely I can no longer see her clothes. All I see is a river of red. I look up and notice her throat has been cut. I run to help her, but suddenly she is gone and I am awake.*

Each dream flashed me back to the time your grandpa told me David had said my dad had killed my mom. *Could it be true? Is that what happened to my parents? Were they dead? Had my relatives given me to Marilyn and James?*

A few answers materialized when I got a call from someone saying she was a distant cousin. She and her husband were traveling through, and David had given them my number. On the phone she explained that they were checking out some family genealogy and wondered if they could stop by for a visit.

When they arrived, I was nervous but excited; maybe she knew something about my past. Before I could ask a question, she started talking about our family tree. She had some paperwork to give me just in case I ever wanted to join the Daughters of the American Revolution.

"You're eligible, you know. Oh, I guess you didn't know that either, but in your bloodline, you are related to a former president of the United States."

"Which one?" I inquired, not terribly interested.

"Rutherford B. Hayes is on your mother's side of the family," she chatted on. "And here are some pictures of your relatives from way back, and this is a picture of your mom and dad with some of your brothers and sister."

As she handed me the photo, I looked, for the first time in my memory, upon the images of the people she said were my biological family. I saw a man dressed in bib overalls with dark curly hair, a tiny woman in a print dress and five kids, four boys and a girl. Some of the children were dark headed, and some were blond like me. My cousin said that they were my father Helmuth, my mother Violette, and proceeded to name the children. She said the picture was taken before the last three, including me, were born.

They were all strangers. I had not a flicker of recognition or memory of any of them. I felt no connection. Not one. I asked her if she had a picture of me as a child, but she didn't. As much as I wanted to believe these people were a part of me, I couldn't. There had been too many lies, and I needed proof. I didn't know what to say, so I mumbled, "So there were eight kids. We sure were a large family."

"Actually," she answered, "there would have been more of you if your mom hadn't been murdered. She was about seven months pregnant when she died."

There it was again, murder. My mom was murdered. *Is that what those dreams were about? Is it possible that Harold had been right those many years ago? What did* David *know about it?* On one level, I wanted to know more, but something inside kept backing up. The cousin didn't volunteer any more information about the murder, and I didn't ask. Our visit came to an end, and she left me with pictures of the people to whom I was supposed to be related.

After her visit, I got to thinking about the information I had received. My name was Grace Ann, the same name that was on the long ago inheritance check from my Grandfather Neuharth. I knew where I was supposedly born. I had names for all the aunts, uncles, brothers, and a sister. David was really my birth brother Rueben. I could find out more if I wanted to. The question was, did I want to?

Another dream perfectly illustrated my inner struggle of wanting and yet at the same time not wanting to know the truth about my past. In this dream I had yearned to see one of my aunts on my father's side of the family, and I was happy when I received an invitation to a reception in her honor after church services. *I sit in the service, feeling anxious as it drags on and on. Periodically people slip out and make their way to the fellowship hall where my aunt is. Thinking I might as well give it a try, I get up. On my way out, someone tells me that I have to wait until the service ends before I can go into the fellowship hall. I sit down but decide to try again. The same scenario plays out two more times. On my third trip out of the service, I demand they let me pass saying, "I have already waited over thirty years, and I have a right to go in there and see my aunt."*

I walk into the fellowship hall and sit down at a table beside her. We are carrying on a conversation when out of the corner of my eye I notice a lady watching me. She looks strangely familiar. Crossing the room to my table, she sits a plate of food in front of me and then holds out a box and asks, "Do you want to see the knife your father used to kill me?"

My heart pounds; it's hard to breathe. I am caught completely off-guard by her question. I don't know what to say. Somewhere behind me a loud voice screams, "You have twenty seconds to make up your mind. Come on, you have ten seconds left. Hurry up, five seconds...four...three!" The voice gets louder and louder as he counts down. I'm trying to think. I don't want to be pressured into something I'm not ready for. I hesitate. Then, very close to my ear, the voice thunders, "I need you answer now!"

I scream no and wake up. I just wasn't emotionally strong enough to face the truth. That dream proved to be as prophetic as it was insightful.

---

*D*ear *G*irls,

I had so many unanswered questions about my past I wasn't sure what to look for. It was like those times when you get a craving for something but don't know exactly what it is. So you open up the refrigerator and search for it. You may take a small bite of this or that just to rule it out. Then you proceed on to the pantry in your search for it. Now you may find it or you may not, but when you do find it, you will know because you will be satisfied. I was not satisfied.

Not long after pastor prayed for me, I sat out on a quest to find the answers I needed. I started with David. Over the years, much of our talk had been on a superficial level but we did have a history together, and I trusted him. After God used him to pray for me the day I almost drove off the bridge, he became more of a counselor, yet he had never mentioned our parents' deaths.

When I told him about the dreams and our cousin's visit, he confirmed everything, and at that point, I intellectually accepted the fact that our mother had been murdered. Actually it was a matter of giving in to the general consensus rather than being fully convinced. I still had no proof.

I had barely begun my search when God sent someone along to help. One of my nieces called me to ask questions about her grandparents, my parents. Of course, I knew less than she did, but together via mail and phone, we widened our search.

When I received the copy of the newspaper article about my parents' deaths, the account was very much like my dreams.

The *Yankton Daily Press and Dakotan* account read like this:

Man Slays Wife Then Takes Own Life in Cistern
Tuesday Morning Tragedy at Helmuth
Neuharth Residence Discovered
When Children Come Home from School

Helmuth S. Neuharth, 45, slashed his wife, Violet, 44, to death with a five inch hunting knife Tuesday morning and then took his own life by drowning in a cistern at their rural residence four miles north and one mile west of Yankton. Sheriff Walter Mueller said today that the apparent murder and suicide took place between 8:20 and 9:06 Tuesday. The time was established by reason of the fact that three of the Neuharth children left for school at about 8:20 and a watch was found on Neuharths body had stopped at 9:06.

The tragedy wasn't discovered until late Tuesday afternoon when the three oldest children returned home from school at 4:30 p.m. The oldest of the three youngsters, Douglas, 14, told Sheriff Mueller that it was a short time afterwards that he went into the bedroom and found his mother lying in a pool of blood on the floor.

Douglas ran to a neighboring farm to report the incident, the neighbor telephoned the Sheriff's office and Dr. R.F. Hubner, county physician, at 5:15 p.m.

Started Search

Mueller, Dr. Hubner and Deputy Sheriff Marvin Van Osdel went immediately to the Neuharth place, decided the evidence indicated murder, and ordered an immediate search of the premises for the husband.

It didn't take long to find Neuharth's body. Someone noticed that the top of the cistern had been taken off and that a rope used for the cistern was lying a few feet away. One of the search party, Floyd Nelson, detected Neuharth head in the water, and the body was then pulled out. The cistern had six feet of water in it, Mueller said.

Three Children Home

Three of the couples eight children-Reuben 5, Grace Ann 3 and La Verne Dale 22 months were at the house through out the day. When their three older brothers came home from school, one of the younger children said they hadn't had any lunch and their mother was "in the bedroom."

The article goes on to say where Dad was employed, where our home sat in relationship to the mental hospital, and that the Neuharth's did no farming on the place. Why that mattered, I have no idea. It also noted that the five younger children were taken to the hospital for care.

I carefully studied the pictures in the paper, the kitchen, a white enamel tea kettle sitting on the wood-burning cook stove, the table, the house, old car in the yard, an out building, the lid of the cistern where my father reportedly ended his own life. I might as well have been looking at pictures in a library book. Nothing looked familiar.

I wrote to the police department in Yankton and requested a copy of their report of the incident. Since it was a closed case, the file had been destroyed long ago. I proceeded on to the coroner's report, which was also a dead end. No autopsy had been done. I finally got a copy of my parents' death certificates. Mom's death certificate stated: "Throat slashed including esophagus right and left carotids, right and left jugular veins. Numerous stab wounds on hands."

*D*ear *G*irls,

*M*y niece and I connected with many family members. Although they filled us in on many details, no one was anxious to talk about the murder. We thought the questions were benign, our relatives did not see it that way. We were often quizzed on why we needed to know these things. Our curiosity seemed strange to them, but we pushed on. I received letters from aunts and a neighbor who lived near us in South Dakota. I received copies of letters written by my mother to her sisters. I always asked if they had a picture of me as a child. No one did.

I did discover a number of other facts...

Your great-grandmother Violette McPherson was less than five feet tall with brown eyes and black hair. She may have weighed about a hundred pounds "soaking wet" as they say. In her pictures she is beautiful and sad. About her girlhood I know little, except that she graduated from high school and won a lot of spelling bees. No one knows for sure how she met my father, but it is believed that the McPhersons and the Neuharths had neighboring farms.

After the wedding, the babies came at regular intervals. Violette was nearly forty years old when the midwife laid me in her arms. Looking into my face, she declared, "I will name her Grace, for by the grace of God I got another girl after having four boys in a row."

Your great-grandfather Helmuth Neuharth was of German descent, short and stocky. His thick black hair was curly and his eyes clear blue. As a boy, he liked to tinker with bicycles, cars, and tractors. Although he worked at the mental hospital for over ten years, he had gone to technical school to become a power-plant mechanic. His large certificate of graduation hung in a frame on our living room wall, along with a wedding picture.

Dad was a full-fledged alcoholic and made wine from the fruit of the mulberry trees that grew near our house. He was given to jealousy, control, and violent fits. Emotional and physical abuse was a part of the relationship between your great-grandparents.

Like many alcoholics, Helmuth Neuharth was a self-centered, self-absorbed man. His word was law, and he flew into a rage if anyone questioned his decisions. The world revolved around him, and we weren't allowed to have an original thought. I don't know if he was predisposed to violence, but it is said that individuals who violently abuse their families can drink for the sole purpose of providing a time-out in which they can blame their behavior on alcohol.

He never wanted anyone to visit us while he was gone, not even family, and Mom feared to leave the house because there would be hell to pay if he found out. For months at a time she went nowhere, and no one came to see her. Her sister-in-law told me she wished the family had stuck closer to Mom when she needed help, but they were afraid of what would happen if they did.

Besides the loneliness, Mother suffered physical and emotional battering because the social structure of her world said she could do nothing about the man who beat her. In those days, women were little more than a man's property, and, like abused women now, fear probably kept her from leaving. Fear of retaliation. Fear of not being able to support her children. Fear of being alone. But by staying she placed herself in a state of suspended animation where no element of the situation could change.

I can imagine her relief each day as she watched him cross the road and jump over the fence to his job at the mental hospital. For a few hours she wouldn't have to be afraid of saying the wrong thing or looking the wrong way or any other multiple unknown infractions that would set him off. When the evening bell rang, signaling quitting time, she forged up her courage to face whatever mood Dad was in when he walked through the door. She never knew if he would greet her with a hug or a fist in the face.

Strangely, it is the possibility of "this time things will be different" that hypnotizes abused women into holding on. That pitiful hope is their undoing. I'm sure Mom treasured every fragment of the times when Dad did something caring for her or the family. Like when he killed the snake ready to strike one of the children or when he took Mom to a beauty shop in town to get a perm or, on a rare sober evening, sang German lullabies about angels to us after we were in bed. These tiny windows of sweet normality in the souls of abusive men keep women hanging on.

Mom hung on even when she had to hide one of her sons because his father frequently threatened to cut off his penis with a hunting knife. She hung on when he beat her so savagely that one of my siblings knocked him out with a cast iron skillet to save her life. That time he was taken off to jail, but Mom dropped the charges and held on to "maybe next time."

*D*ear *L*ibby and *R*ylee,

*A*s I worked in the garden this morning, cutting off the tops of purple onions and picking salad greens for lunch, I thought about how hard it must have been to feed a family of eight kids. I am sure my mother did her best, but I found out that half a sandwich and a bowl of soup was often all we had for a whole day. The two goats provided milk and butter, although never enough, so the small garden she planted each spring was the mainstay of our food supply. That is, if you don't count the fact that the older boys used mice to get food for the family.

Poor children seem to be born with the knowledge that everyone in the family is responsible for trying to get food. My brothers were resourceful, but the use of mice happened quite by accident. It began during lunchtime at school when one of my brothers slipped his hand into the paper sack holding his half sandwich and a mouse scurried up his arm, jumped to the floor and ran past the teacher. We were used to mice, so it didn't bother my brother, but the teacher reacted as you might suspect.

After calming down a bit, she confiscated the sandwich, telling him it was now dirty and had to be thrown away. When he loudly protested that he was hungry, the teacher asked his classmates to share their lunches with him. My brother was given more food during that lunch hour than anyone in our family had eaten in a whole week. He ate his fill and brought the rest home.

From time to time, the other school-age children took

turns using this method to obtain food. It was a ploy that worked well for them.

---

*D*ear *G*irls,

*E*ven in the most dysfunctional families there are things that can't help but make you laugh. Another amusing family story has to do with your great-grandfather and Charles Lindbergh. Charles Lindbergh was the first person to fly a solo, nonstop transatlantic flight from New York to Paris in a single-engine airplane. This feat made him world famous.

Years later, tragedy struck the Lindberghs when their twenty-month-old son was kidnapped. Every newspaper in the country carried the story and pictures of the baby as well as the prime suspects. Flyers were posted everywhere proclaiming, "Wanted: Information as to the Whereabouts of Charles A. Lindbergh Jr., Son of Col. Chas. A. Lindbergh."

This is where Dad came in. About three months after they were married, a little boy who my grandmother McPherson had been taking care of came to live with Mom and Dad. It was about the same time the Lindbergh baby was kidnapped.

Who knows what caused him to do it, perhaps seeing all the newspaper articles and wanted posters gave Dad what he considered a "brilliant idea." But then again, Father was an alcoholic, and possibly, while on one of his binges, he got to thinking that he needed to explain why they suddenly had a two-year-old little boy. So he began spreading rumors that the child was really the Lindbergh baby.

Granted, the blond, curly-headed little guy had a remarkable resemblance to the missing Lindbergh child and was near the same age. Not only that, the picture of one of the people being questioned in the kidnapping was a maid in the Lindbergh home named Violette Sharpe. In her picture, this lady looked very much like mother. Same first name, same coloring, same hairstyle, and same tiny build.

Apparently no one in town took Dad's claims seriously, or the locals were amazingly adept at keeping secrets, because, to the best of my knowledge, the FBI never showed up. Dad might not have been so liberal in spreading this ridiculous story had he known that handwriting experts had determined that the person who wrote the ransom note was of German descent. Of course, Dad wasn't known for his rational thinking.

Yet, at least one person fully believed Dad's story. Years ago, as I researched our family history, I called Aunt Hilda (Dad's sister) to ask her who the baby's father was, and she answered matter-of-factly, "Oh, he was a famous pilot with a plane called the *Spirit of Something* or other." I was speechless.

"Surely you don't mean Charles Lindbergh?"

"Yes, that's him!" she emphatically declared. Thirty years later, Aunt Hilda still believed that Dad had told her the truth. That's family for you!

*D*ear *G*irls,

*H*ere are some excerpts from letters written by your great-grandmother. In them you will see glimpses of her heart as well as her daily life. This one is to her sister Lottie.

> Dear Lottie all,
> Hope you got home O.K. It sure is raining here today. My garden looks good all except my okra. It isn't coming so good. I'm working on the quilt Earsel [another sister] gave me. I haven't been up to the folks for 6 years. In fact I don't even know where they live.
> Helmuth went into town yesterday morning and came home drunk as usual. He always promises me he will get us strawberry plants and things, and when he comes home he never brings anything. We wouldn't even have had Christmas if the Salvation Army didn't give the children clothes and gave us our Christmas dinner.
> Suppose Helmuth will go into town Sat. night and won't get home until sometime Sunday morning. He must be doing something besides drinking because he sure gets mad when we want to go along. Well it is about mail time so must quit and get this mailed.
> Children have to walk down to railroad track and get some fuel so I can bake today.
> With Love, Violette and children

And in a couple of letters to a family member who had taken my sister in to live with them:

Dear Maxine, Jack, and Elaine,

Got your letter today, so I thought I better answer it. I finally got my quilt finished, so now I am taking some of my white flour sacks and making sheets out of them and want to take some of mine and Elaine's clothes and cut them down for Grace.

Grace says to tell Elaine her baby doll did come home yesterday. [This may have been the doll one of our uncles brought Elaine before I was born. A brother says he remembers it was dressed all in red including the cap and shoes. Possibly Elaine sent it back to me.]

Don't know if you can read my writing or not as LaVerne is sitting on my lap. Sure wish he could walk as it wouldn't be so much work. He is over a year and a half but has been sick so much. He crawls and walks around chairs. Even when he was real small we had a lot of trouble with him. I think he will start walking before too awful long. Helmuth won't take him to the doctor and not even Grace when she had pneumonia. He said we couldn't spend money on a child. He always goes when he even has a little scratch.

We sure use a lot of flour, got three pans with flour coupons and sent after another last week should be getting it before long. Well better quit and have supper ready by the time the kids come home from school or else there will be some blue smoke rollin.' Glad Elaine likes it there.

Love, Aunt Vi and Uncle Hel kids.

Dear All,

Can't get Elaine's report card in letter so

will have to wait until we get a bigger envelope. Helmuth left for his folks. Not long after you came up for Elaine someone reported him to the Board of Charity that the children weren't getting enough to eat, and when I told him about it he blamed the boys. Am almost positive it was the neighbors. The teacher goes down to the Salvation Army and gets eats for the kids unbeknownst to Helmuth. She has a hot plate over there, and she cooks them things at her place.

You have to be awful careful what you write in your letters as he can sure make a mountain out of a mole hill, and he has to read every letter I write. Only reason I wrote this is because he has gone to his folks.

I haven't been off this place since before Thanksgiving.

Love, Violette

Eventually we set up a reunion of sorts with five of my brothers, including David/Rueben. Like most family reunions, everyone carefully danced around all unpleasant topics. The murder-suicide never came up. They talked and acted as if our parents had lived and died a normal life and we, their perfectly adjusted grown-up children, were simply having a little get-together to talk over old times. In a picture we took that day of the six of us, I am gazing off into space with a detached look on my face, as if to say, "Who are these people, and why am I here?"

When I went to see my sister, it was the same thing. She really tried to help by making meat pies baked to a golden brown, using our mother's recipe. She told me when she was smaller (probably before so many kids came along) that mom had invited her class over to the house and prepared this recipe for all of them, and they loved it. My sister also sang a song in German that Dad had sung to us. She kept asking, don't you remember such and such? Or this or that? Neither the song, recipe, nor her memories rang any bells for me.

One of my aunts sent me a white china cream pitcher that had been removed from our house after Mom died. On the front of the pitcher is a scene that looks like it may have been hand painted. The picture is of a barn with a red roof and yellow walls. There are green bushes on either side of the barn and a tree in the background with no leaves. I still have the pitcher, but to this day I have no recall of ever seeing it before it was given to me.

Only one memento from my past affected me at all. My oldest brother sent me a picture of Mom standing by a storage shed next to a goat. I already had pictures of her, but this one was different. When I looked at that picture, fear gripped me. I immediately slammed it face down on the table. Something about her face or the shed or the goat went through me like lightning from hell. It was horrifying. I could not look at that picture without being terrorized.

The search did help me put together pieces of the puzzle from my more immediate past. My cousin's comment about my mother being seven months pregnant kept surfacing in my mind. One day I made a connection to something that had happened during my own pregnancies that I hadn't understood at the time. Before Abigail was born, I woke up one morning crying and was unable to stop. Sorrow engulfed me. Inside I felt a dark aching emptiness as if the most horrible event had taken place. For no apparent reason I cried and cried and cried from the time I got up until the time I went to bed. I was seven months pregnant.

With Hannah, I was two weeks overdue. A dreadful conviction came over me that she just had to be born before the first of the month. I simply could not carry her past then. Near panic I pleaded with the doctor to go ahead and induce labor. He told me to wait another week. I asked people to pray. Everyone thought I was anxious because she was overdue, but I knew it had to be something more. Something terrible was going to happen to both of us if she wasn't born before the month ended. My mother and her unborn baby died near the first of the month.

---

*D*ear *G*irls,

*A*lthough I had what most people would consider ample proof about my past, I still wondered why I couldn't feel anything. Had I stuffed my emotions so far down that I was incapable of connecting to my own family? What was missing? Nothing seemed real. Not the murder. Not the newspaper headline. Not even the death certificates. If all this was true, where was the grief? Except for the isolated incidents when I went into emotional overload looking at the picture of my mother with the goat and my pregnancies, I had felt nothing. Then one night all that changed.

Harold, Hannah, and I had gone out to eat at a buffet-style restaurant. When the cashier asked how many in our party, I answered, "Three."

When she charged me for three adult buffets, I said, "Oh, one is for a child." But she insisted it was my fault because I did not tell her. Once it was rung up, she could not correct it, so I paid for three adults and let it go.

When I reached for a plate off the buffet table, Harold grabbed my forearm and snarled, "Don't you ever embarrass me like that again!"

Fear shot through me. A volcano of suppressed emotions erupted as my mind spun backwards to another time and another life when another man had grabbed a woman's arm and said those exact words to her. I was four years old and in the kitchen with my mother... the knife... the blood... my baby brother screaming... my baby doll dropping to the floor.

Anger, terror, fear, bitterness, guilt, grief, and helplessness ripped past all the other torturous issues I had buried under and slammed me with the full impact of what had actually happened. Like molten lava, agony flowed through my soul as the dissociate memory broke into consciousness. I had never felt pain like this before. *Oh God! My Mommy! Why did he do it? Why? Why?*

At that moment, standing in a buffet line, I relived the whole murder and finally knew it was true. I had been there. I had seen it.

It is early May. Flowers are blooming. I had picked a handful of purple ones for Mommy. The big kids are off to school. My brother Reuben is outside climbing trees or something, and Daddy went to work before I got up.

My baby doll and I are at the kitchen table eating breakfast with Mommy. Mommy looks pretty. Daddy took her to town yesterday and got curls in her long black hair. We are happy today; Mommy hummed a song while she cooked breakfast. Baby LaVerne is in his high chair banging the tray with a spoon. He wants breakfast too. I am Mommy's big girl helper, so I tell him, "Wait a minute. It's a comin'!"

The kitchen door bangs open, and Daddy is there. I didn't know why Daddy is home. I look at Mommy; her eyes are big. Daddy's face is red. He hits the table, making the dishes rattle. He's screaming bad words at Mommy and grabs her arm, jerking her up. As she pulls away I get a sick feeling in my tummy. I grab my baby doll and run into the corner. Daddy is reaching for something on top of the stove—it's his knife, the big knife he uses to skin rabbits.

Mommy screams Daddy's name as he moves toward her, waving the knife through the air. She backs up to the bedroom door, holding her hands out in front of her belly. Dad slashes at her arms, making blood come out her skin. He points the knife at me and screams, "Grace Ann! Get out of here!"

I drop my baby doll and run outside around the house to look in the bedroom window where Mommy is hiding. She is crying. Daddy kicks in the door. Her hands are getting things red—the bed, the walls, the window. Daddy yells, and Mommy screams. Mommy's pretty hair is messed up. Daddy keeps jabbing at her with the knife. She is crying. He jumps at her and swings his arm through the air, I see her neck open up; a river of red comes. I don't want to look, but I can't look away. The river goes on and on, covering the whole front of her dress. I call her name, but she stops moving. She falls to the floor, the red river is wetting her pretty hair.

I hide in the trees and cry and cry, holding my hands on my mouth so Daddy won't hear. He yells at me when I cry. I cry until I have no tears. I am cold and hungry. I want my mommy. I curl up in the dirt and wait for her to come. I don't hear nothin' but the birds. I stay very still. I feel a hand on my shoulder. I want it to be Mommy. My brother says he is going for help and I should stay there. I close my eyes and see the red river coming out of Mommy's neck. I try not to close my eyes. I start crying again. I am Mommy's big girl helper, but I can't help her. I am not quite four years old.

Somehow I found myself at the table with food on my plate. A steel band of horror tightened around my chest; I willed myself to breathe. Numb with shock, I sat out the meal in silence while Hannah and Harold bantered back and forth. I was so well versed in hiding my emotions that no one around me knew anything was wrong.

The next morning, at the end of the service, Pastor called me forward for prayer. I wish I could tell you what he prayed, but I cannot. All I remember is that I had the urge to scream "Mom" as loud and as long as I could hold out that single-syllable word. The silent scream came forth from the very depths of my soul. After the prayer the overpowering emotions no longer had a death grip on my heart. The only thing left was grief. It had been thirty-two years since the murder, but for the first time, I believed my parents were dead.

---

*D*ear *G*irls,

*A*fter remembering the details surrounding my parents' deaths, the grief lasted several months. Ultimately I went to a psychologist for counseling once a week for six weeks. I knew Harold would never approve of anything I did to get better, so I didn't tell him.

The psychologist was quite interested in my story and asked if he could use the filmed interviews as a teaching tool. I'm not sure what he was going to teach out of them because about all I got out of it was him suggesting I write a letter to my parents and tell them what was in my heart. I wrote something like, "I never got to say good-bye, so now...I will say good-bye and let you go," and then I destroyed the letters.

At the end of six weeks, I was a bit tired of all the psychobabble, so at my regular counseling sessions I told the psychologist that I now believed Dad had people mad at him because he was German and that somehow he killed Mom for the benefit of us kids, so we could have something to eat. Then I let him know I was done with counseling. It is possible that he figured I had flipped completely out, because his only question was, "What are your plans for the rest of the day?"

I expected he was worried that I might try to kill myself, so I set his mind at ease by saying, "Oh, I have an exercise class to go to with my daughter, groceries to buy, and tonight we will go to church." He seemed satisfied with my answer, shook my hand, and wished me well. That was the end of my stint with the psychologist.

I went about my life as I had before, seeking information about my past. Among the things I learned included what happened after the bodies were found. We children were taken to Sacred Heart Hospital for examinations.

Nurses tried to get me to talk, but I was mute until they brought in my five-year-old brother, Rueben. I grabbed him and began crying hysterically. When I wouldn't turn him loose, they let him stay the night. We curled up together in one bed.

When my relatives showed up to claim me, I was standing at the foot of the bed clinging to Rueben. A nurse tried to pull us apart, but upon hearing they were only taking one of us we began bawling and holding each other even tighter. Loosening my frantic grip, my uncle and aunt led me down the hall, away from the only familiar person left in my shrinking world. The nurse held my brother so he couldn't run after me.

The trip to my aunt and uncle's was traumatic. Curled up in the back seat of the car, they told me I sobbed unrelentingly, calling Rueben's name. They tucked me into bed on the couch and while I slept, my kind uncle and aunt decided that it would not be right to separate me from Rueben. They placed a call to the hospital and told them that at ten o'clock in the morning they would be back to claim him as well.

In Yankton, the other children were split up and taken in by different people. The local newspapers continued to carry the details of the murder-suicide embellished with full-page pictures of our parents and our house. Within a week, this article appeared in the local paper:

Morbid Curiosity Brings Visitors to Neuharth House

Morbid curiosity drew numerous people to the Helmuth Neuharth rural residence Northwest of

Yankton over the weekend, Sheriff Walter Muller said today. The house was the scene of a murder-suicide tragedy last Tuesday, when Neuharth slashed his wife's throat and then took his own life by drowning in a cistern.

The intrusion became so bad that the Sheriff declared he was forced to bar the front door and put up a sign warning that trespassers would be arrested.

Mueller stated that when he visited the place on Sunday that there were several cars with curious visitors looking over the premises. The door to the house had been broken down, not only that, but the sheriff found that intruders had gone through everything in the house, leaving things in disorder. Many personal belonging were missing.

These many years later, I am sitting here on the screened porch in Arkansas gazing at a copy of that fifty-eight-year-old newspaper article. It's hard to imagine strangers going through our house just to see my mother's blood on the floor and looking around for souvenirs. One of the things missing that day was my baby doll that I dropped when Dad ordered me out of the house.

As I reread the article, I noticed below it is one of those lines of useless information newspapers use to fill space. It said, "Minneapolis is exactly midway between the equator and the North Pole." On the day that bit of trivia was written, I was exactly midway between a really bad life and hell on earth.

---

*D*ear *L*ibby and *R*ylee,

*M*y new home was a one-room apartment atop a store. Rueben's coming eased the loneliness. Although Uncle Glen was mother's brother, I had only met him and Aunt Inez once before. Living with them was so much better in many ways. For the first time, we had plenty to eat, and they took very good care of us, but the apartment was far too small for a family of four. Within two weeks it was decided that we needed a home with younger parents.

Because our plight was so widely publicized, the district attorney in Yankton had received nearly three thousand letters from all across the United States wanting to adopt any or all of us. There were many possibilities, but ultimately the family and the court decided that Rueben and I would go to a couple living in California.

Aunt Inez and Uncle Glen had heard about them from their daughter-in-law, who had heard about them from a waitress named Eleanor. This Eleanor went on and on about how wonderful these people were. The wife had gone to Bible college and had been the chauffer for Aimee Semple McPherson, the lady evangelist who founded the Foursquare Church. The husband was a policeman. They had a real nice home. Good people. Their only child had died soon after birth, and they wanted children very, very much. They were willing to allow our family to visit us anytime.

Letters and phone calls between the couple and Aunt Inez soon convinced her that they would be the perfect parents. Of the three thousand applicants, James and Marilyn

Hoskins were considered the cream of the crop. And so arrangements were made for us to go to California.

Since it was over a thousand-mile drive, our uncle would take us halfway where his son Kevin would meet us. We'd stay with Kevin and his wife until the adoption was legalized. On the endless road trip, Rueben asked at regular intervals continuously, "Are we there yet? Are we there yet?" He was excited, while I continued to be disoriented and fearful. I had heard them say that Uncle Glen was only going to take us halfway, so I got it in my almost four-year-old head that we were going to be dropped off by the side of a road and left. I could picture us alone out in the middle of nowhere, waiting for somebody to pick us up. I watched the empty miles roll by, wondering when he was going to pull over and make us get out of the car.

When we got to the halfway point, our cousin Kevin was already waiting. He was just a few years older than my biggest brother and talked nonstop, keeping us entertained so the last half of the trip passed faster. Before we knew it, we had arrived, and Kevin's wife was greeting us at the door. Rebecca was nice and happy to see us, bragging on my big blue eyes and telling Rueben he was a handsome boy.

They had a three-bedroom house in a nice neighborhood. Country kids that we were, Rueben and I had never seen houses so close together. We shared a room since the other bedroom had already been turned into a nursery for the baby they were expecting in a few weeks.

Kevin and Rebecca made us feel like a part of the family and in truth, would have adopted us if Kevin had not been in college. To us, they were a revelation. We had never been around adults who were fun and seemed to enjoy our company. They played and laughed like kids and took us everywhere. We had many new experiences, including eating at a restaurant where we were introduced to the wonders of hamburgers, fries, and cokes.

One day, Kevin asked Rueben if he wanted to help him wash the car. Following Rueben's excited, "Sure!" Kevin carefully explained about the two buckets of water they were going to use.

"Rueben, this first bucket is clean water. I dip the sponge into it and wash the car down. The second bucket I use to rinse out my sponge before I dip it back into the first bucket and continue on, got it?"

Feeling important to be given a grown-up job, Rueben nodded his head as if he fully understood the concept of washing a car with two buckets. Kevin said, "Okay, buddy, you do this side, and I'll do the other."

After a bit, Kevin checked to see how he was doing and found Rueben happily and efficiently washing the car with dirty, gritty water. When he saw Kevin's face, he knew he had messed up, but instead of getting mad, Kevin began to laugh, and they ended up in a big water fight.

About the second week into our stay with Kevin and Rebecca, I heard them discussing something in hushed tones. Fear still danced around the edges of everything that happened, so, hearing the whispers, I begin to worry we would have to move again.

They had asked us to play outside and to knock before we came back into the house. It was a pretty day, so staying outside was not the problem. The problem was the scent in the air. The curtains to the house had been drawn, so we couldn't peek, but the smell of fried chicken and something chocolate baking drifted through the open window. After about what seemed an hour, we were starving!

When Kevin finally came to get us and we had made our way into the dining room, we saw it had been decorated with colorful crêpe paper and balloons. There on the table was the fried chicken and a chocolate cake. Along the side of the table were lots of beautifully wrapped gifts.

Both Kevin and Rebecca shouted, "Happy Birthday, Grace!" I was told I stood in silence as if totally caught off guard.

"Grace," Rueben whispered into my ear, "today is my birthday, but you can't let Kevin and Rebecca know that. Just go along with them; they are trying to be nice to us."

With that, my very grown-up, six-year-old brother yelled, "Happy Birthday, Gracie!"

I felt so special that day. It was the closest thing to a real birthday party I ever had. Fried chicken and chocolate cake were my favorites. The gifts included pretty dresses and a baby doll. As I opened gifts, Rueben acted as delighted as if they were for him. It was a foretaste of the kind of man he was to become. For a few brief weeks, my brother and I came very close to having a normal life.

---

*D*ear *G*irls,

*T*he day following the party we met our new parents-to-be. Rebecca carefully dressed us up to impress our callers. She curled my blond locks and let me wear one of my new birthday dresses. Rueben's unruly hair was slicked back with a bit of Kevin's hair oil, and he had on new clothes too. When she stood us in front of her dresser mirror, we giggled at our reflection, thinking we looked real pretty. By the time the couple arrived, we were sober and scared. Standing close together, hands locked, we were determined not to be separated again.

James and Marilyn Hoskins were in their early thirties. He was about six feet tall with blond hair; she was a smidgen over five feet with short red hair. They talked in pleasant tones and made a point to include us in their conversation. He told Rueben he was a policeman, and she said she worked at a restaurant that served really good food. Upon leaving they hugged us and said, "We will be back soon and take you to your new home in California."

Although the thought of a policeman daddy and all those hamburgers and fries sounded okay, we did not want to go anywhere. We were happy with Kevin and Rebecca, but within a month the couple had filed the petition to adopt us, and arrangements were made for us to stay with them until the court date. Once again, we were on the way to another life.

Rueben said he did not remember much about the next few months. Both James and Marilyn worked a lot, and they had someone come in to care for us. He did, however, remember our day in court. The petition had been filed, and it was now up to the judge to decide whether or not they were to become our parents. A lot of the proceedings were over our heads, but when the judge granted the petition for our names to be changed, we heard that loud and clear. Rueben told me that I got mad and whispered to him, "I like my name! My mommy named me Grace Ann! I am Grace Ann! People can't take your name!"

But they did.

It was decreed that I would no longer be Grace Ann. Since our new parents wanted us to be named after them, I became Marilyn Sue, and Rueben became James David. It was further decided that all our previous records were to be sealed to protect our birth parents. In retrospect, this seems strange, considering our birth parents were already dead. Even back then the judicial system had a few holes in it.

Within a matter of a few months, we lost our parents, our home, our brothers and sister, and our names. For me, an even bigger loss was coming... on the way home from the courthouse was when I lost my memory.

Even with all I had discovered, something was still missing. My ongoing quest for living relatives dwindled until I was down to one last cousin. To my surprise, she held the answer I had been searching for.

When I inquired about the murder, she could only tell me about the funeral. "I remember seeing your mom in her casket. There was a gauze bandage around her neck." When I heard that, a peace came over me. I had spent so much time and energy searching for what an adult would want to know, when it was really the child in me that had been hurt and needed reassurance. To a hurt four-year-old child, a bandage is everything. For someone to put a bandage on my mom was a sign that someone cared enough to let the healing process begin.

I had found 'it.' Not long after that, I legally changed my name back to Grace Ann.

---

*D*ear *G*irls,

*A*s I was moving toward wholeness, your grandpa's nerves began bothering him more than usual. Swearing he couldn't sit still for any length of time, he was like a yo-yo, up and down all day long. If we went out to eat, he'd bolt through his meal and go sit in the car with the motor running until we finished. As objective and emotionally unattached as I was to him, I found it interesting that he had no problem sitting in a theater for the duration of a movie but could not stay in church for the entire service. When his panic attacks intensified, he started taking more and more tranquilizers until he was addicted. At one point, the doctor tried to take him off gradually. For most of the week, he sat in a corner of our living room and cried.

Other than drugs, his chosen release for his inner demons was to get behind the wheel and drive. He declared over and over, "My nerves are shot, and I have to get out of here!" There were times I wanted to say, "So go!" but that was not how it worked. Hannah and I were required to immediately drop everything we were doing, pile in the car, and ride around with him until he calmed down.

During this time, the company he worked for announced layoffs. They had listed the number of people from each department that would be leaving, and it looked as if Harold would lose his job. The company also offered early retirement to those who were eligible and set up a service to help those being laid off to find employment elsewhere.

Your grandpa had been really worried about the layoffs. He wanted me to help him update his résumé, but I had prayed and felt God tell me that he would not be laid off. Of course, he refused to believe it and argued that in order for him to stay, all of the people in his department who were offered early retirement would have to take it. In addition to that, one other person would have to volunteer to quit.

His spiel went like this: "You have no idea what you are talking about, Grace. You don't know the men I work with. They would never accept early retirement. For someone else to just up and quit, well, that isn't going to happen either. But if you are so sure, then I just won't be looking for another job. What happens will be on your head."

One by one, those who were offered early retirement took the offer. Harold was now one person away from being laid off. To his surprise, one of the guys went into the office and asked if he could get severance pay if he left. The answer came back yes. Harold did not get laid off.

A couple of months later, one of the guys who had changed jobs told Harold people were needed at the automobile plant where he now worked. It would require a move. Did he want an application?

"Well, Mrs. Smarty Pants, should I take the application?" he asked mockingly.

After praying, I told him to fill out the application and put the house on the market. The Realtor told us that with so many layoffs it would probably take us six months or more to sell. I assured him that the house would go fast. In four weeks, we had a cash buyer.

So how did I know? My theory is that I was able to

hear the voice of God because I had shut out most of the other voices around me. There is something about living in your own silence that makes it possible to hear a still small voice from inside your spirit. I also believe God was positioning me so that I would be prepared for the events on the horizon.

We found a small duplex to live in while we looked for a home. Usually, finding a house was a relatively simple task for us. By now we bordered on being professional house hunters. But this time three of our offers fell through. We purchased land but couldn't get a house built. Busy and determined to do what we had always done, I failed to ask God why we were having so many problems. Had I been paying attention, it would have saved me a lot of unnecessary stress. Three months after we signed the mortgage on our new house, we found out your grandpa had brain cancer.

---

*D*ear *G*irls,

*H*e had been working on a machine at the factory when he banged his head on a door that had been left open above him. Ordinarily this would have been a minor accident since he didn't break the skin or even have a bump. An hour later, when he reported the accident to the plant nurse, his hand was having tremors.

At the hospital, the preliminary X-ray showed dark spots on his brain. The next day was a round of exams, EEGs, blood tests, and a brain scan. We were sent home, and that night I woke up being hit by Harold's flailing arms. Jumping out of bed, I turned on the light to find him in the midst of a grand mal seizure.

I was told he had a number of cancerous brain tumors. When he bumped his head, he had hit one of the tumors and dislodged it, which caused the tremors and seizure. The doctors gave him no hope. Harold stayed in the hospital, and I went home to call the family and tell the girls.

After the doctor pronounced his death sentence, Harold told me, "If I had known that at the end of my life you would be called upon to be my caregiver, I want you to know that I would have treated you as good as gold, but now it is too late for that." Yes, it was too late for that, but I set aside everything and with tunnel vision embraced what I had to do. My one goal was to keep Harold alive.

The next year was a whirlwind of going back and forth to doctors, selling the house, and moving into an apartment. As his mind and speech soon became seriously affected, I had to make medical decisions for him.

Emotionally, I was right back where I had been with Marilyn. If I made a wrong decision, he would be dead. *There are four different kinds of chemo he could take. Which one? What do you think about trying surgery? What about this? Here are the side effects. You could take him to this hospital for veterans.* My head spun. I told our pastor I felt like I was in the middle of a minefield and didn't know what each step would produce. He said you should feel that every day and should run everything past the Lord.

I did learn that God can give you an amazing amount of wisdom to do what you have to do. For instance, because his words did not always come out as they should, it was difficult for him to tell me what he needed. One day, he asked me for a blanket. When I gave him one, he told me that it was not a blanket. So I asked him, "What do you want to do with a blanket?" He opened his mouth and pointed to it. That narrowed down the field considerably. It had to be medicine, food, or drink. I told him it wasn't time for medication, but I would go into the kitchen and bring him back something to eat and drink. He told me it wasn't a blanket, but it would do.

Another time, on a routine visit, I told the doctor I thought his medication was too high. He explained to me that if it were too high he would be having certain symptoms, which he was not. I maintained I still thought the medication levels were too high, and at my insistence, they drew blood and checked it. The doctor was surprised that his meds were getting into the toxic levels.

Living close to Harold's family was a blessing and a curse. His father, Ted, would come by to sit with him to give me a break. As usual, his mother was another story. When Harold first got sick, she tried to make a deal with me that she would help me take care of him if I agreed to sign over to her our house and all insurance money that I would get if/when he died. I declined her kind offer.

Then she called and said that Harold wanted her to have our only vehicle, a new van only a few months old. Again I said, "I don't think so." But she went on to explain, "I checked at a dealership, and most people apply for disability insurance, so you wouldn't be out any money. You could give me the van and go buy another one." I told her we didn't sign up for disability insurance and besides I needed the van to get Harold to his appointments. Of course that was all irrelevant.

When I sold the house, she got mad at me for daring to be so presumptuous as to keep the small profit from the sale. It was my duty to give it to Harold's brother. I began to think that compared to his mother Harold had been a walk in the park.

About a year after his diagnosis, your grandpa began having trouble breathing. His tragic life ended in an ambulance on the way to the hospital. He was forty-five years old. They took me into a room and showed me his body. I didn't cry. I had no grief left.

Sometimes it makes me sad to think of what might have been and his lost potential. He was like so many other people; he had the cards stacked against him from the beginning and never found his way out of the maze of emotional damage.

*D*ear *G*irls,

    *A*fter the funeral, a couple from the town we had lived in for six years said Hannah and I could live with them for a while if we wanted to move back. We took them up on the offer and stayed two weeks before finding an apartment. By this time, Libby, your mom and dad had been married five years and lived on an army base. So, fifteen-year-old Hannah and I set out to make a life for just the two of us.

    My personality began to change after Harold's death. I had been so controlled and subdued most of my life that it appeared that I had no personality. No passion. No happiness. No sadness. No strong opinion or emotion about anything. Abigail admitted to me years later that when she was a teenager she would sometimes try to make me mad just to break through the shell I seemed to be encased in. One day, after her dad's death, I said something funny, and she exclaimed in surprise, "Why, Mom! You have a sense of humor! It's a little off the wall, but it's there."

    There had been times during my ordeal that I felt that the real Grace Ann was much different from who I had become. In retrospect, I think that my motivation to research my past was actually to find the real me. When I asked family members what I was like before, they just said that I was a quiet content child—not the answer I'd hoped for. Still, in the back of my mind I thought that somewhere deep down inside I had a fun-loving side, fearless and full of hope. I longed to see that little girl who knew how to laugh and play, but I did not know how to find her. Little did I know that she was hiding deep in my soul, waiting to come out and participate in a life that, up until now, she had only been able to observe from a detached state.

I read somewhere that when a person disappears into a fear and self-rejection mode, the body takes on a profile of death. That made me think back to when your grandpa and I were first married. When the doctor took my blood pressure, he asked me if I was sure I was alive. My blood pressure was 67 over 47, with the norm being 120 over 80. He said I needed to wear an ID tag, because if for any reason a paramedic checked my blood pressure, I would be treated for shock. My body was manifesting the state of my soul—shock.

I have learned that our soul is our animated self, the seat of our personalities, the spark through which we manifest who we are. Abused and traumatized since birth, I had frozen all feelings (because it hurt too much to feel) until I had no self. In many areas, my soul was so out of commission no one could see me. The real Grace became invisible.

Back when we renewed our wedding vows, I called and reserved the church fellowship hall for the reception. Now, mind you, I had been teaching Sunday school there for about three years, and the church only had 150 to 200 people in the whole congregation. When I went to double-check on the room, they told me I couldn't have it because Marilyn Cramer had already reserved it. "But I am Marilyn Cramer," I protested. They did not believe me until I showed them my driver's license.

Then there was the lady I met at church after your

grandfather died. Frostie and I became great friends, but in the beginning, although I sat next to her in service, afterwards she had to really work at remembering me. Later, she said that even after two months she was still going to the extent of taking notes on my physical appearance, but try as she might she could never recognize me. I was a nonperson, wounded beyond recognition.

I wanted my life. I wanted more than just a flare-up of an off-the-wall sense of humor and the ability to stand up for myself every once in a while. I wanted Grace Ann, whoever she might be. I had made some headway, but my recovery had been in jagged pieces, few and far between. It would take some serious God moments to set me truly free. When that day finally came, it was like finding a long-lost love. For the first time I really began to love and appreciate who I was created to be.

---

*D*ear *G*irls,

*L*ife without Harold was peaceful. We laughed more. I remember the first time after his death that Hannah and I went out to eat at a restaurant. The waitress had just taken our drink order, and while she went to get them, we both commented on how it would be so good to sit down at a meal and not have Harold spill his drink all over. Because of his tumors, he could not judge distance and often knocked over his glass. We had come to expect it. When the waitress brought our iced tea, she accidentally spilled one, and we both got tea on us. The waitress fully expected us to get mad, but we both started laughing hysterically.

To be better prepared to support Hannah and myself, I started college. Numbers had always come easy for me, so I signed up to take accounting. A few months later, I bought a house near the campus. We went to church every service. I felt I was doing well, considering everything, but my old nemesis fear still had me in his grip. I had lived with him so long his presence was barely noticeable to my conscious mind. Yet deep down, the poison Marilyn had deposited in my heart, and Harold had reinforced, was still very much a part of me. At the time I wasn't aware of the source, but I still had a deeply rooted belief that if a mistake was made it could cause someone's death.

There is a scripture that says out of the abundance of the heart the mouth speaks. Sometimes we think that we are over things, but our unplanned words tell a different story. Once I noticed a mistake in the church bulletin and pointed it out to my friend Frostie by saying, "The church secretary made a fatal mistake on the bulletin." When Frostie asked me why I used the word *fatal* for a simple error, I saw it. I still felt every mistake could be fatal. It did not just go away when Marilyn killed herself and Harold died. In fact, their deaths proved my theory. To my shattered soul, I had failed to keep either one of them alive.

This possibility of messing up caused me to be super vigilant around everybody. Once while visiting Abigail, I got chilled from an open window. Rather than asking her to shut the window, I put on a sweater. A friend of hers was there and later asked, "Why didn't your mom just shut the window?" Her answer told the story, "Because she was afraid to tell me she was cold. She thought it would hurt my feelings."

This fear had controlled my life, and I was tired of it. When I felt God was saying, "Let's get rid of it," I asked Frostie if our church had anyone who did counseling. It didn't, but I got a referral to a Christian counseling service at another church seventy-five miles away.

This therapist was a woman, so I was more comfortable with her than I had been with the psychologist. She started off our session with a prayer inviting the Lord to be part of the process of healing and asking him to supernaturally erase from my mind anything that was not helpful.

I brought up the murder-suicide first, thinking it was the source of my problems. I told her just the facts without emotion, as if I were reading it from the newspaper article and ended with, "I always feel responsible for everybody else's life."

She remarked, "That is an unusual reaction to watching someone being murdered."

Over the years, I had blamed many of my issues on the

fact that I was an orphan, but as she probed the real truth of why I felt I had to keep everyone else alive surfaced. It took a few more sessions for me to bring up Marilyn, and then it began to make more sense to her. Ultimately, over a period of time, she was able to convince me that it was not my fault that Marilyn had killed herself.

About three sessions into my six months of counseling, I complained that most of the sermons I heard didn't make sense to me. She looked at me for a minute and then said, "Honey, I am so sorry that I did not recognize this before. I have to start talking to you differently so you can understand." She then asked if I ever watched *Star Trek*. When I nodded, she continued, "You are like Mr. Spock on the show. You remember he was half Vulcan (pure logic, no emotions) and half human. The part of Spock that almost always came through was his pure logical side. Seldom, if ever, did you ever see his human side. That is you, Grace. You have suppressed your emotions for so long they are almost nonexistent."

I could see she might have a point. Emotionally damaged people can bury their feelings until they literally do not feel life. The fact that I might lack emotional nerve endings made sense.

"You probably have a hard time with sermons because most sermons appeal to human emotions, which you do not understand." She ended the session by offering to translate parts of sermons that interested me into pure logic.

Girls, can you picture a conversation between Captain Kirk and Spock as to whether Spock should have emotions and what they are good for anyway? Well, that was the conversation I had with Frostie after that session.

"Frostie, the counselor said today that I am sort of like Spock on *Star Trek* and I don't have any emotions. Is this true about me?"

"I doubt she said you had no emotions. She probably said that you showed no emotions. But I know you have them, or you wouldn't have changed your name back to Grace. You just haven't been allowed to show them for so long."

"Do I really need to have emotions like the rest of you people?"

"Huh? What is with this 'like the rest of you people?' Grace, having emotions is normal. You especially need to let them out before something explodes. You've suppressed them for so long."

"Oh."

"Be forewarned," she continued, "emotions do sometimes get in the way of spiritual things. I think many times we say that God wants us to do something or other when it's really just our emotions speaking."

"So what you are saying is I need them to keep from exploding. But if I get them, there is a chance that it will be harder for me to hear the voice of God."

I mulled all this over for a while, and one Sunday night at church I told Frostie I had made up my mind. "I want healing for my emotions; I guess it's time I become like you all. Will you pray with me to have emotions?" Together we went to the altar and prayed. God honored my prayer, and for the first time in forever, I began to feel things like other people.

---

*D*ear *G*irls,

*I*n one of my last sessions with the insightful therapist, she said it was now time to forgive the people who had hurt me so badly. That was a big one. I read somewhere that sometimes we don't want to let go of our pain because we fear that letting go will change the fact that it happened. But just because we forgive them does not mean they were not guilty. Forgiveness isn't denial. It simply meant I am not going to carry the hurt around anymore.

I had to undo some faulty teaching on the subject, but once I got it through my head that forgiveness does not equal trust, I was ready to take the next step in my healing.

Since that day, I have learned that forgiving a person is not the same as tolerating their behavior. Christian author Lewis B. Smedes writes, "When we forgive evil we do not excuse it, we do not tolerate it, we do not smother it. We look the evil full in the face, call it what it is, let its horror shock and stun and enrage us, and only then do we forgive it."

Another insight came from Archbishop Desmond Tutu, who said, "Without forgiveness, there's no future." I really wanted a future. I was ready, and so was God. That day in my counselor's office, when I bowed my head, I felt his presence fill the room. It was as if the Holy Spirit was swirling around me as I forgave everyone from my past. When I was through, their sin had dissolved in dust behind me, and I was ready to go forward.

My friend Wanda wrote a poem out of her own life that summed up my experience that day.

Forgiveness
You hurt me
You took my last bit of dignity
Shredded it in my face
Saying things I can't repeat
Then you laughed at me

You hurt my children
Took their innocence away
And left a wounded soul
Where children use to play
Then you said it was my fault

Yes, you hurt me
But this day I am healed
As I hand you forgiveness
I loose your hold upon my soul
And I walk away in Peace

*D*ear *G*irls,

*R*ylee, when you were little, I remember how you use to love to help me with the fresh-picked peas from the garden. You and I would sit around the table and peel off the outer shell. I can still see the surprise in your eyes each time you found the perfectly formed peas inside the pod. My healing was much like our pea pods.

The counselor, being led by the Holy Spirit, helped peel away my outer shell, setting me free from my past. The healing of my emotions opened a whole new world and I became the happy child I had never been, and Frostie was there like a mother to enjoy it with me.

She had started a singles group in our church and drafted me as her assistant. One day, I told her that I never got to fly a kite. So she planned a singles event around kite flying. When I mentioned I had always wanted to go to an ice cream social, we had one. Growing up, I was never allowed to see a baseball or football game, so the group also went to a baseball game together. I was living my youth over as a forty-four-year-old woman, and I was having a ball.

We had changed pastors at the church we attended. This new pastor was someone who just lent himself to being teased. One of our traditions in that town was that when we got a new pastor we forked his yard by sticking as many plastic forks into his lawn as we could without being caught.

We singles had just finished our old-fashioned ice cream social when we decided to welcome the pastor. Parking our cars on a side street, we jumped a drainage ditch, which was no easy task as all the girls were wearing long dresses, and split up the packages of forks. We were having a hilarious time sticking forks all over the lawn when Pastor's car suddenly came around the corner. Running like crazy, we made it across the drainage ditch and to our cars without being seen. Unfortunately, we only had enough time to leave about 150 forks.

That was the first of our fun with our new pastor. We had only begun. Memorial Day weekend Frostie, Hannah, and I took a two-day trip to Hot Springs, Arkansas. Our new pastor was from there and he was always bragging about Stubby's Bar-B-Q. He would go on and on about the delicious aroma and describe in detail the mouthwatering flavor of brisket dripping in a sauce which was "sweet but not overly spicy." His Stubby's commercial usually came at the end of a long Sunday morning service when the congregation was hungry enough to eat a hymnal.

While in Hot Springs, Frostie had the idea to order some barbecue from Stubby's, have it frozen, and take it back on the plane with us. I asked them to make up a receipt with Pastor's name and address on the top, then add a $150.00 delivery charge to the bill.

Once back home, we got someone he didn't know to deliver the food. She was to tell him he ordered it and now he needed to pay the bill, including the delivery. We had also bought him an Arkansas Razorback cap, which the lady wore on her head backwards. Of course we were in a car a safe distance away watching, although we could not hear.

When he appeared to be getting agitated, our delivery girl let him off the hook. She gave him his brisket, the cap, and a note from Frostie. It said something to the effect that one of the groups in the church had done this as payback because he always mentioned barbecue when the congregation was most hungry.

The following Sunday morning I overheard his wife say she doubted that it was really from Stubby's. "After all, nobody would go all the way to Arkansas to play a trick on us." That was the perfect opening for me. I walked up and said, "Sorry I couldn't be here last weekend, but here is a bulletin from the church I attended." When she looked at a picture on the back, her expression was priceless. She knew the pastors in Arkansas.

I really got into the practical joking side of the new me. Before I knew it, I was spreading the laughs to my college campus. There was one professor I picked on the whole semester. He was teaching a night class on accounting using a computer. I did not particularly want to be in this class. I was totally unsure of computers and did not know if I could handle the class or not. So I though I might as well make the best of the situation.

Every week I did something different to him. It started out when I placed a can of cashew nuts on his desk. I knew for a fact that he liked cashews, so I told him, "I'm getting my bribe in early. I need at least a D in this class to graduate." The next week I paid for a pizza and asked them to deliver it in the middle of class. Then I made up a teacher's survival kit as a gift. It contained a pair of scissors which I labeled, "Old Fashioned Paper Shredder"; an erasable red pen "Because teachers do make mistakes"; and a pair of Groucho Marx glasses as a disguise to wear to class when he announced one of his pop quizzes. He was a good sport about all of this and took it in stride.

Not only had the fun-loving child appeared, she brought with her the impulsive teen who flew off to San Francisco on a whim so many years ago. One day I decided to take Hannah to Florida and signed up for a Disney vacation package. This package included our airfare there and a rental car, a three-day stay at a Disney resort with free tickets to Disneyland, Epcot Center, MGM studios, followed by four days on the Big Red Boat cruise to the Bahamas.

The plane ride, the rental car, and the drive to the resort all went well. Then we checked in, and they gave me verbal instructions to find our room. We followed their directions as best we could, found a parking place, and then decided to grab a bite to eat. Crossing a bridge to the eating island, we ordered up. After dinner I noticed that we had gotten turned around and there were six identical bridges leading to the restaurant. Now we had to find the car and the room.

We circled the complex for a while, but everything looked alike and none of the numbers matched our key. After an hour, we gave up and started looking for the car. Not an easy task to walk through six massive parking lots in search of a white rental car that matched the sticker on the bumper with the sticker on your key ring. After another hour we finally found it.

I was trying to drive back to the office for more directions but somehow got on a freeway ramp and had to figure out a way to get to the motel again. At long last I marched into the office for the second time and demanded, "Please help me find my room!" They told me how smart I looked, and handed me a map. It was dark. I was tired and in no mood for another search. By then we had already been looking for our room for three and a half hours.

As we walked back out to the rental car, I told Hannah to get me a beach towel from the suitcase. While she was doing that, I looked around for a tree branch. I put the beach towel around my shoulder like a shawl and used the branch for a cane. When the next person came along, I hobbled up to her and asked in a quavering voice, "Could you please help a poor widow lady find her room?" She said, "Sure, ma'am, be glad to!" A few minutes later we were turning the key in our lock. The next day I asked for a room closer to the office.

---

*D*ear *G*irls,

I had come a long way in the year and a half since your grandpa died. Like many people in recovery, after I reached a certain feel-good point I got complacent about the rest of my healing. After all, I was 70 percent better, and it was wonderful. My self-talk went like this: "Everything is so great now, and this is such an improvement why not settle in here for a while?" Yet God and I still had some unfinished business.

While going to the Christian counselor, I had shared with her how upset I was because a lady in the church called me a widow. She said I got mad because I felt more like a divorcée than widowed. Widows are always pictured as someone who is in mourning all the time. They constantly talk about their late husband and savor every memento of their life together. She was right. I felt I had nothing to savor and precious little to talk about. I just wanted to move on.

Given my attitude and the fact that I was trying to make up for all I had lost over the years, even the people I was around all the time never guessed I was a widow. Hannah had people ask her where her dad lived and if she saw him often.

When I told the therapist that I had not cried one time since Harold died, she gave me an assignment. I was to get a teddy bear, call it Harold and tell it all that was in my heart. Well I got the bear and took it home, but I could not stretch my imagination far enough to think of him as Harold. A cuddly teddy bear had zero to do with my memories of him. I wanted to do the assignment, but this was just not working for me. There had to be another way to heal the memories I had of Harold.

The next Sunday morning, Pastor made a comment in his sermon that struck me the wrong way. He said that once you attend a Pentecostal church then you can never go back to a community church. I found out that morning that my past issues with pastor's telling me what I could and couldn't do was not really past. He made me mad. What flashed in my mind was the fact that Harold's dad was now pastor at a community church. My stubborn streak kicked in, and I said to myself, "Well, we will see about that!" I told God that I was going to visit Ted's church if he had no objection. I did not hear God say no, so I went.

I had not seen Ted since the funeral. In a lot of ways your grandpa resembled him. Ted was a version of what Harold would have been like had he been healed. I called his sister-in-law about service times, asking her not to tell him and his new wife I was coming. We arrived about thirty minutes early, and while we waited I wondered why I was there and almost decided to go home.

Ted and his wife Sandra pulled up and went inside the church. When I walked in, Dad held out his arms and hugged me, saying, "My daughter is home." I sat down toward the back beside Sandra. After greeting a few other people he made his way back to me and began asking me questions. The questions were nothing major, just if I was doing okay, was I still in school, etc., but I could feel myself getting defensive. He was so much like his son it was as if Harold was interrogating me instead of a nice man asking about my life. Dad sensed my anger and backed off to greet other members of the congregation. I heard him tell someone that I was Harold's widow. At the word *widow*, I could feel the anger in me turning to rage.

Girls, as you are going through your lives, and you think you are over something, pay attention to the red flags that flare up in the form of emotional reactions that are totally out of proportion to the immediate circumstance. If someone, or something, can push a button in your soul, you still have a problem. I definitely still had a problem. I was mad at Ted because he had said something that reminded me of Harold.

Service started and someone else was preaching. Ted was sitting on the platform facing me, but I didn't want to look at him. I felt a major wall between us. The guest preacher was long winded. When the altar call was made, I was still angry enough to refuse to go forward. But when the service was over I found myself going forward and telling Ted, "I came for prayer because I've never cried since Harold died and for the past several weeks God has been telling me it's time to let go. But something inside won't let me release what needs to be released."

He gave me a hug and said, "God will work it out." Taking my hand, we knelt together to pray. At this point, it was as if your grandpa and I were there as a couple praying. This was something I always wanted to do, but there was no way Harold would.

Ted prayed, "Father, I know how badly Grace has been hurt, and I ask you to show her how much you love her and assure her, Father, that you will never hurt her."

It was everything I needed to hear Harold say. Then he looked into my eyes and said, "Grace, God has something great in store for you." There, at the altar of a community church, while holding hands with God's chosen stand-in for Harold, I began to cry, and he cried with me. It was a holy healing time.

They invited us to spend the night, and so after having lunch with Sandra's daughter we went home with them. Toward the evening, Ted decided to make some popcorn, and I followed him into the kitchen to get a drink of water. After finishing my drink, I reached out to hug him. He took me in his arms, and as he went to kiss my cheek, I laid my head on his shoulder, causing him to accidentally kiss my neck. Harold had only done that one time in all the years we were together, and it had been a rare special moment. I just stayed in Ted's arms, breathing in the scent I had always associated with Harold. He told me he loved me, and I told him I loved him too and I missed him.

The microwave signaled that the popcorn was ready, and the hug was over. We went back into the living room and visited a short time. Then everyone went to bed. I felt as if I had spent the last five hours with Harold and he had told me everything I needed to hear. Through Ted, God supernaturally healed all the memories of our marriage and set me free.

I had been told that when your husband dies you feel an extra connection with heaven that others cannot feel. I don't know about that, but after that time I felt connected to the real Harold and loved him as he might have been.

---

*D*ear *G*irls,

About a year later, after the healing of my memories about your grandpa, I graduated from college and got a job doing payroll for a local company. I continued going to church and doing things with the singles. I was happy. I liked my job, and my employers liked me. I laughed a lot. I swung through my days carefree and so very contented to discover God really loved me and took care of all my needs. It was wonderful to get to know him as a "Father to the orphans and a husband to the widows."

I still did impulsive things. One day after an extremely hard week of work, I came home and told Hannah, "Hey, Mom is tired, so I took a vacation day. Let's go to the amusement park and ride all the rides." And we did.

I also stepped into a ministry of my own. With another lady, we began a fellowship group for the widows in the church. We got together once a month to eat and bounce ideas off of each other. For instance one lady asked, "Should I sell my house now that my husband is gone?" Each of us told her what we did and why. If any one of us didn't want to go somewhere alone, another volunteered to go with her. One Christmas, we made arrangements to have dinner together at a restaurant located in a fancy Victorian home. I rented a limo to pick us up. For most of us, this was a first; we felt like royalty or at least red-carpeted movie stars.

Then, much to my dismay, God threw a monkey wrench into my finely oiled works. I began to sense in my spirit that he wanted me to get married again. My first reaction was,

"Oh great! Why are you trying to punish me?" I did not want to ever marry again. Life was good. I liked not having to ask a man before I bought a new dress or have to get someone's okay to take a spur-of-the-moment trip.

My second reaction was resignation. Although I couldn't get excited about messing up a good thing, I eventually came around to the outside possibility that I just might get married again if Mr. Right came along. Since I had learned to pray about everything in detail, I decided I needed a name for my future husband. If I had to have one, I did not want to refer to him in my prayers as the guy, so I decided to call him Steve. I prayed about this Steve person off and on for three years, asking God to bless him and guide him in his life. But as time passed and he was a no-show, I began to think I had missed what God was saying. That was fine with me; I almost breathed a sigh of relief.

About that time, I got a letter from a wonderful lady we had met way back when your grandpa and I were first married. As the years passed, we stayed in touch with her and her husband, visiting each other when we could. Ella was the kind of person every pastor wishes he had ten of: a devout prayer warrior, a Sunday school teacher who visited each one of her students in their home once a year. She also supported and wrote to a number of missionary families all over the world.

So I got a letter from this awesome woman of God, and in essence she informed me that her older son was available. *Oh great, the minute I give up on Mr. Right, I get this!* I had met Bruce several times during the course of our friendship with Ella and her husband, so it wasn't as if he was a complete stranger. I had also been hearing about him for years in his mom's letters.

Well, girls, one thing led to another, and before I knew it, we were talking on the phone...a lot. When he mentioned that he was going to see his folks for Thanksgiving, I felt led to invite myself to join them. Hannah and I flew out the day before Thanksgiving. I had a fleeting inclination that we should wear costumes on the plane; I could be a pilgrim and Hannah an Indian maiden, but I thought better of it, as I didn't want to freak him out right away. I ended up wearing a new pair of jeans, a white blouse, and a bright red vest. I was feeling pretty chic until a lady walked up to me in the airport and mentioned that I might want to take the sticky tag off my backside that announced to the world what size jeans I wore.

Bruce was laid back. From the beginning, he accepted me for what I was and wasn't put off by my uniqueness. He had no control issues, nor was he the nervous type. So, when he proposed to me that weekend in the cab of his pickup truck, I said yes. It really was a special moment for both of us; we could feel the presence of God wrapping us in peace. The following Valentine's Day, we were married. Years later, Ella told me that she really wanted to name Bruce Steve but his dad wouldn't let her.

---

*D*ear *G*irls,

*M*y brother Rueben died a few years after I remarried. His lungs kept filling up with fluid, but I honestly thought he would be healed. He confided in me that he had asked God whether or not he was going to make it and God's reply was, "Well, do you want to?" Reuben opted out and asked God to take him home. He was fifty-eight years old.

Reuben always loved God, but stayed a firm believer that the message had to be taken beyond the walls of the church. He chose to do that in various ways. First, he tried ministering in prisons but soon realized that his personal story made even hardened criminals cry. After that he tried other outreaches and finally landed on his favorite, a hotline ministry. He really enjoyed taking calls from people who needed help. Whether the person was suicidal or just wanted to talk through a problem, Rueben always had a way of helping them.

In a way, I was a bit envious because he seemed to get over everything earlier than I did and move on to a place of real ministry. Yet inside Rueben was still hurting. As the years progressed, we talked about the murder and our feelings surrounding it. Yet even as we shared it seemed, we were competing to help fix wounds the other had sustained. Although both of us went through the same thing, our outlook and the way it affected us were very different. Rueben could never get past the stage where he felt guilty about not doing more to help our mother. He was only five years old at the time, but nothing I said ever convinced him he wasn't somehow at fault for her death.

All his life, Reuben felt he was in a barrel careening down a hill. It would stop just long enough for him to catch his breath and start rolling again. He was tired of being tossed about and just wanted to go home. He felt that he had missed out on many things in life.

Sometimes it is the little things that tend to hurt the most. In my case, even as an adult, the fact I had never had a real birthday party cut deeply into my heart. The little girl in me yearned for a party celebrating my very own birthday. Sometimes it hurt more than the death of my parents. As a rule, people do not understand how a small oversight can have such a huge impact. In the end it was the little disappointments that hurt him most. I believe my brother died of a broken heart. He simply could not go on.

Before he died, he sent me these words of wisdom: "We are all products of how we were treated when we were very small. Whatever we have now took root in the soil we were planted in long ago. But unlike plants, we are not stuck to those roots. We can move and we can change. Our often tortured pasts need not be our destiny. Our capacity of healing and repair is greater than we realize." Rueben decided to go on to heaven and complete his healing there. I choose to stay here.

*D*ear *G*irls,

I do not want to leave you with the impression that when I married Mr. Right we rode off into the sunset in his pickup truck and lived happily ever after. We are happy, but along the way there have been challenges. Rueben's death brought on a great sadness. I missed my brother and spiritual counselor. His passing left a huge hole in my heart.

Sometime after Rueben went home to be with the Lord, our pastor preached about putting the past behind you. That sermon really nailed my ongoing healing. He said, "Maybe something that happened in your past taints the way you see things. You may be arguing with someone about one thing, but it really has to do with something else." Even now, I have to continually watch over my soul's tendency to react from the past.

When people hear my story, they are amazed that I ever ended up with any kind of normal life. All I can say is it is by the grace of God. As I look back over my sixty-plus years, I can boil it down to four things that I needed to get here.

The first one was a quality decision to be healed. A quality decision is one in which there is no turning back. Without that, nothing would have ever changed. As the old saying goes, I got sick and tired of being sick and tired and decided something had to give. The cost of doing nothing was too high of a price to pay.

The second was tenacity. Like Jacob in the Bible, I got to the point where I said, "God, I am going to hang on to you and not let you go until you heal me." Like a pit bull, you hang on and on no matter what things look like from where you are now. God was my only option. I did not have anyone else to cling to or confide in. I could not depend on myself since I had no resources to accomplish that feat.

The third thing I needed was honesty between me and God. He already knew what I was thinking and feeling, but sometimes, like King David, I was honest enough to get mad and question him. I found he could handle my anger and did not fall off of his throne when I yelled at him. But after all the anger, I still held on to the belief that he could fix the things in my life that needed to be fixed. Honesty with God meant I also had to be willing to be honest with myself.

Fourth, I renewed my mind with the Word of God. When I read something in the Bible or someone preached a sermon that touched my heart, I wrote it down. It didn't matter if I didn't understand why something touched me, I just wrote it down and hid it in my heart. At the time I heard the story of the city of refuge, I did not understand why it impacted me, but years later it was a place to park my guilt about Marilyn's death. I also used "For God hath not given me a spirit of fear, but of power and of love and a sound mind" and lived in the truth that God looks out for widows and fatherless children. By doing this, I was reprogramming my soul and replacing the negative core beliefs with positive ones.

I cannot tell you that it is easy to get from so much pain and hurt to wholeness and peace, but the trip is worth it. Many hurting people want to jump in and just fix their symptoms to make the pain go away. Father God wants to not only take care of the symptoms but also get to the core of the issue. That takes time. A quick fix would be nice, but it took a long time for me to get so messed up and I have learned to give God equal time to bring me to wholeness. I am patient with myself, and I am patient with God. I am a work in progress, and God is perfecting that which he has began. My day-to-day life gives him plenty of material to work with.

Through it all, I have found him faithful to lead and guide me into his perfect plan for my life and give me peace.

*D*ear *G*irls,

A few years after I married your Grandpa Bruce, we moved to our farm in Arkansas. Probably by your standards, I don't lead a very exciting life, just one of peace and quiet. I like it. We are seventeen miles from a Wal-Mart, but during the summertime the closest town has music on the square. We take our lawn chairs and sit in the blocked-off street listening. Tonight a group played jazz and old-time songs from your great-grandparents' day.

As I wrap up these letters, it is autumn. Our garden is now barren, getting ready for the winter solace. We have put down some compost to replenish the nutrients it has lost. Toward the back of the house, six cement pillars mark the start of the room addition to enlarge the borders of our house. In other areas, I am enlarging the borders of my life.

During my morning walk, I noticed some of the trees kept their brilliant green color; others have turned different hues of gold and red. As I head up the gravel driveway, the rooster is crowing, and the fallen hickory nuts roll beneath my feet. The air is fresh and clean.

Across the way, I see the apple tree that produced plenty of apples this year for canned applesauce and apple pie filling. The tree looks odd as it is bent over at a forty-five-degree angle, not from the abundance of fruit, but from the fact that two cedar trees had also made their home at its base. The cedars had done their best to crowd out the apple tree, so it bent forward to reach the light it needed to survive. We have cut down the two cedars, and I have been told that with a little pruning the apple tree will again learn to stand straight and tall again and produce much more fruit. Got to be a lesson there somewhere...

The trees on either side of the path usually provide a canopy of shade on my walk. Today their fallen leaves have spread an oriental carpet of color under my feet. Streams of sunlight dance through the branches illuminating my path. God is good to me.

The creek that winds through the property sometimes only contains a small trickle of water; other times it overflows its banks. Today it is dry, but I notice the once-jagged edges of the rocks have been smoothed out from years of water washing over them. God has washed many of the rough edges of my life into smooth round stones so that most of the time even floods run smoothly on and I stand firm.

I turn around to head home and notice that from this vantage point my journey has been a slow steady uphill climb. From here on, the walk will be easier. Back at the house with a steaming cup of hot chocolate, I am thinking of final words of wisdom I could pass on to you.

This is what I have come up with. Know where the line is that separates your past from your present. Know that what has happened to you or what you have done does not define who you are. Only God can define who you are, and he sees you perfected. The way you perceive things becomes your reality, so ask him to help you see yourself and others through his eyes.

Get a picture of how really big God is and all the things he has for you. The biggest problem facing Christians today is the fact that they do not know they are beloved children of God and he is on their side. Get to know him up close and personal. Know that you have a right to his promises. If you don't feel you have a right to something, you won't take it... even gifts from God.

Ask God each day if there is anything you need to know about what's coming up and if there is anything he wants you to do for him, so you can live your life by destiny rather than by default.

If the same circumstances keep repeating in your life, ask yourself why and begin to take action so they don't have a chance to keep you in bondage. You will always meet great resistance when you are leaving a place of bondage. Stick up for yourself. If you always try to avoid a conflict, you'll never be an overcomer.

When life gets rough and you feel like giving up, hold on tighter to God than ever before. Your attitude has everything to do with how your life ends up. If you think you can, you can. Set goals for yourself and go after them in spite of your circumstances.

Always be true to who you are. Don't try to be something you are not. Do the things in life that you have a passion for and don't worry so much about trying to master those things that you are not interested in. Your gifts are in you. Learn to value them and yourself as a unique one-of-a-kind gift sent to the earth from God. Unless you feel good about yourself, you will always be disappointed.

When asked to do something, always take a few minutes to really think it out instead of making a snap decision. Never make decisions in life that you are not comfortable with thinking it will get better. If you are not comfortable, it probably means you are compromising somewhere when you shouldn't.

As you grow older, your life seems to come full circle. When your personal healings and God moments happen, use them to gently guide others to find their own path through misery. You too can turn negatives into positives and end up with something more useful than bad memories... experience.

In closing, I will share part of a letter I received from your great Aunt Adeline, my dad's sister. When she wrote this, she was 101 years old. Perhaps her advice to me is the best possible wisdom I can pass on to you girls.

> Dear Gracie,
> Read the Word of God as if you are searching for a hidden treasure. There won't be anything in eternity that is not like God. You never go wrong by giving yourself to the scripture. The purpose of life is to produce fruit to eternal life. You are never a peacemaker if you insist that you are right. These are some nice thoughts to think about.

Yes, Aunt Adeline, those are some nice thought to think about. Thanks.

Girls, I want to leave you with one last thought from an unknown author. "You are daughters of our family history—but you will be mothers to a new generation. I have faith you will do it right."

Note from Wanda

At this writing, I have never met Grace. A couple of years ago, her daughter gave her a copy of my book *The Search for Peace: A Woman's Guide to Spiritual Wholeness*, and we began to e-mail back and forth. She shared with me that she had been trying to write a book for years and had almost given up. As a nonfiction writer dealing with women's issues, her story intrigued me. I asked her to send me what she had, and when I saw the overview I knew I had another assignment from God.

Along the way, she has sent me pictures, old letters from her relatives, copies of notes in her mother's handwriting, and newspaper accounts of the murder-suicide deaths of her mom and dad. Everything I read verified her story.

Over the next nine months, our e-mails filled cyber space. She sent me her memories; I e-mailed back questions and questions and more questions until the full picture came into view. Then I weaved it all together into the format we had decided on, letters to her granddaughters. I sent her my version, and she made corrections and additions, and we would begin again. About 789 e-mails later, we had written a book.

My belief is every woman has a story, and writing down that story can be a powerful tool to bring about inner healing. Helping Grace with her memoir has brought about more healing in her life and mine. They say you write what you need to read, and so I did. Thanks, Grace.

As we wrote through her life, I was continually delighted to see Grace come more and more into her own unique persona. She never ceases to amaze me, and sometimes I just have to laugh out loud at her antics. Just last Sunday I got this e-mail from her.

> Dear Wanda,
> This morning, as I was going through my closet "with lots of clothes but nothing to wear," you know how that goes, I thought about the dress that I bought this week. In an effort to find Libby a *Little House on the Prairie* outfit for her Harvest Festival, I placed an ad in the paper for an Amish dress and apron. I had always thought that I would have made a good Amish lady. I love the way they dress and how they strive for a simpler way of life. As I contemplated wearing the dress and apron to church, Bruce said that I should do it. So here I am, dressed for church in an Amish outfit (no head covering). In certain ways, I think that the last letters inspired me to do something out of the ordinary for me. Get out of the box so to speak.
> Love, Grace

All I can say is, "You go, Gracie girl! You go!"

Family Secrets Authors' Bios

Grace Ann Neuharth has lived *Family Secrets: Letters to my Granddaughter.* This is her story and her first book. She believes there is a place in the world for a book that shows clearly that God can fix the most impossible situations. Grace's story will help many people move beyond survival to victory. In fact, it already has.

Grace has found peace and contentment in living the simple life on a farm in Arkansas as God has been preparing her to reach out to others who have been wounded, orphaned, or abused. She has also realized that it is never too late to walk in the calling God has upon her life.

She can be contacted at thelifeofgracie@gmail.com.

Wanda Winters-Gutierrez specializes in creative nonfiction that touches the reader at their deepest level and delivers "aha moments" in abundance. Her work is touching lives around the world and is often recommended by therapists, pastors, counselors, other authors, and motivational speakers. Her book *The Search for Peace: A Woman's Guide to Spiritual Wholeness* is being used in women's prisons, halfway houses, and shelters for abused women as well as a study book in assorted women's organizations.

She is available to hold meetings, workshops, and retreats concerning women's issues, journaling to wholeness, writing your story, and other subjects that enable women to discover the life God created them to live.

On a personal level, Wanda loves the outdoors and daily walks in the desert near her Southwest home or on her family's mountain in Tennessee.

Her email is wpeacejourney@aol.com.

You can also find her on these Web sites:
tiptopwebsite.com/wpeace
http://www.ahamomentbooks.com

listen|imagine|view|experience

AUDIO BOOK DOWNLOAD INCLUDED WITH THIS BOOK!

In your hands you hold a complete digital entertainment package. Besides purchasing the paper version of this book, this book includes a free download of the audio version of this book. Simply use the code listed below when visiting our website. Once downloaded to your computer, you can listen to the book through your computer's speakers, burn it to an audio CD or save the file to your portable music device (such as Apple's popular iPod) and listen on the go!

How to get your free audio book digital download:

1. Visit www.tatepublishing.com and click on the e|LIVE logo on the home page.
2. Enter the following coupon code:
   e760-7bc8-c2b4-fd8c-7290-6dc2-432a-8db2
3. Download the audio book from your e|LIVE digital locker and begin enjoying your new digital entertainment package today!